Winning Golf

Winning Golf

Peter Chamberlain

Johnston & Company

Copyright © 1985
Nordbok International, Gothenburg, Sweden

Line drawings: Reg Hager

We would like to thank The Golf Society of
Great Britain for its permission to use the text
on pages 62 – 63.

Printed and bound 1988 by
Grafedit Spa, Azzano S. Paolo,
Bergamo, Italy, by arrangement
with Graphicom, Vicenza.

ISBN 91-87036-12-6

CONTENTS

INTRODUCTION *page* 7

Chapter 1 BUILDING YOUR OWN SWING *page* 9

Chapter 2 UNDERSTANDING BALL FLIGHT PRINCIPLES *page* 35

Chapter 3 PUTTING *page* 65

Chapter 4 UP AND DOWN AROUND THE GREEN *page* 79

Chapter 5 IN TROUBLE AND HOW TO GET OUT *page* 93

Chapter 6 YOUR GOLF ROUND *page 111*

Chapter 7 THE MENTAL GAME *page 123*
by Lars-Erik Sandler

Chapter 8 THE PHYSICAL GAME *page 133*
by Rolf Wirhed

BIBLIOGRAPHY *page 156*

INDEX *page 157*

INTRODUCTION

In 1887, Sir Walter Simpson had the following to say in his golf classic, *The Art of Golf*, about the mysterious movement we call the golf swing: "Do I maintain, then, the reader may ask, that everyone ought to have the same style? By no means; on the contrary, for you or me to model ourselves on a champion is about as profitable as to copy out *Hamlet* in the hope of becoming Shakespeare.

"On the other hand, there is no more fruitful source of bad golf than to suppose that there is some best style for each individual which must be searched out by him if he is to get the best results out of himself. In a broad and general way, each player ought to have, and has, a style which is the reflection of himself—his build, his mind, the age at which he began, and his previous habits."

Simpson's was among the first of a multitude of books aimed at easing the growing pains of the aspiring golfer. Since then, an estimated nine hundred titles have been published. Some of these purport to "sell" the secret of golf; some, written by successful players, tell how they have made the big time; while just a few are based on a more analytical approach to the game. Of the last-named category, the most outstanding is a report of a five-year study commissioned by the Golf Society of Great Britain in 1963 entitled "The Search for the Perfect Swing". The authors, a group of golfing scientists, borrowed a leaf out of Sir Walter's book by not analyzing players first and the swing afterwards. Instead, they considered the physical actions involved in striking the ball. This enabled them to construct a model swing. Then came the difficult part of their work, the "matching" of the model to the human being. The result of all this was, to cut a long story short, that a lot of solid facts were established and these have been of great help in teaching and in other areas of the game.

Sir Walter Simpson's observations nearly a century ago are in agreement with the findings of the G.S.G.B.: so long as we golfers remain members of the human race and continue to differ from each other in matters of age, physique, mental make-up, education, etc.; our way of playing golf is going to be a very personal one.

The model golf swing lies at the end of the rainbow, but you already have your very own swing method somewhere inside you. To develop this "best-for-you" golf game is an exciting challenge, and the results will depend, to a large extent, on the level of your ambitions—perhaps modified by the amount of time you are able to dedicate to practice and playing.

You may be reading this book because you have been given it by an understanding spouse, a sympathetic golfing friend, or have even invested your own hard earned cash in pursuit of golf's holy grail, so let us without further ado go to "work", bearing in mind that old Scottish saying:

"Golf is not a matter of life and death, it is much more serious."

Chapter 1
BUILDING YOUR OWN SWING

"**N**OTHING SUCCEEDS LIKE SUCCESS" is a theme that I would like you to keep in mind throughout the initial learning period. Let me explain why. In order for you to enjoy your instruction and practice sessions, and thereby improve your chances of progress, it is important to experience success. Most of us like a challenge, but we soon tire if we fail too often and don't have a system to fall back on. That is why we are going to put together our game step by step. First of all, we build up a "for-you" natural golf swing. Each step in this build-up is to be crowned with a certain amount of success, which will give you more and more confidence as you go along.

STEP ONE: We start at the end — The putting swing

Your ultimate goal in golf is to see the ball drop into the hole. When it does, you will feel a sense of achievement (even of relief!), and this good feeling is important to your psychological well-being. So let's take out the easiest club to use—the putter—and half a dozen balls onto the putting green.

At all times during this swing-building program, body balance and comfort must be given priority. A *natural* body stance is paramount for a simple and personal swing.

Many of the ingredients of our finished swing are incorporated in the simple movement we are now going to make, and they are a darned sight easier to develop now than later. So let's take it nice and easy, relax and remember—enjoy it!

Your golf game should not only be filled with relaxation and enjoyment, but also with rhythm, and rhythm is the thread that will run throughout the swing-development program. It is easy to learn and remember a movement if it is set to rhythm. Many of us dance a waltz only once or twice a year, but as soon as we hear and feel the rhythm of the music, our "muscle memory" swings us into action. The movement is "programmed" into our memory.

Rhythm and relaxation are friends and work well together. Rhythm and tension are the opposite and do not. We are going to examine the effects of tension, both physical and mental, later on in our training program. But for the time being we shall build immunity to tension by training in such a way that we will follow a pattern of successes.

STAGE ONE

Hold the club out in front of you with your left hand. (If you are left-handed, hold the club in your right hand.

You will discover the best personal position after you have held the club in the outstretched position for a while and adjusted it to suit yourself.

The best way for you is the way which allows you to support the club with the minimum of tension in the muscles of the under arm.

All the instructions in this book are for right-handed people, so all left-handers will have to reverse my instructions where applicable.) You must now support the weight of the clubhead in a natural way and with the steadiest hand position you can achieve.

Your thumb should lie down along the flattened top of the grip.

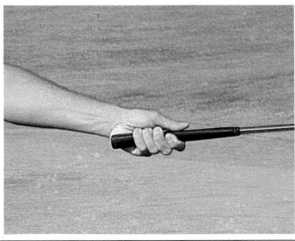

The last three fingers
should clasp the club
firmly into the hand.

Now lower the club to the ground, positioning it with the center of the sole (the underside) flush with the ground. It is important that you are well-balanced and comfortable during this pre-movement position, which in golf is called "the address".

Now that you have lowered your arm to allow the clubhead to rest on the ground, your upper body has probably bowed slightly forward, thus changing your balance slightly. Your body weight has now moved slightly forward and down towards your toes.

Adjust your position by bending the knees slightly to create a more "sitting" position, with the body weight evenly between right and left foot and between toe and heel. It is very important not to allow the club's position to steer the body's address position. "Sit" comfortably, allowing your left arm to hang as relaxed as possible while still supporting the club. You may need to move the clubhead closer or further away, but this is correct—the club's position should not dictate the body's address position.

STAGE TWO
Place the six balls in a line, leaving about 6 inches between each. Address the ball nearest you with the putter's "sweetspot" directly opposite and about half an inch away from the ball. (The sweetspot on a putter is shown in the circular photograph, below right).

Using the same movement as previously, swing the arm and club back and then through the ball, stopping at the end of the stroke for two or three seconds before moving on to the next ball.

CONGRATULATIONS! You have just had your first success at golf—you hit six balls in a row without missing one. And what's more, the chances were good that you struck the ball with, or very close to, the perfect striking area (the sweetspot) on the clubhead. Big deal! you might say, but it beats missing the ball at every second shot with a driver, taking a good deal of God's earth and risking a pulled muscle in the process! Learning to play golf will be fun if you follow this logical system of crawling-before-walking-before-running. Move on now to *Stage Three* and your next success.

Try to strike the ball on the same point with the club blade (*see pages 66–67.*)

SO FAR
We have now started
1. to experience a left-arm dominated swing;
2. to feel a balanced back-and-through tempo;
3. to establish a movement *through* the ball towards the target.

The above three points are common factors in the golf swing, whether it is a simple putting swing or a full swing movement with a wood.

STAGE THREE
Take the six balls to a hole on the putting green, or to a putting cup if you are indoors. Place one ball 12 inches from the hole's nearest edge. Now take two ball markers or small coins and put one halfway between the ball and the hole, and the other in the center of the front edge of the hole. You now have a straight line between the ball, the markers, and the back of the hole.

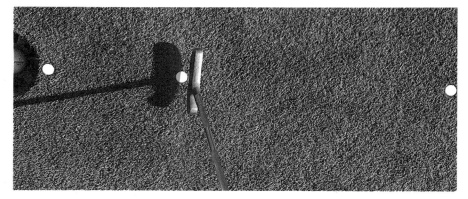

With the left-arm-and-club pendulum movement you learned at *Stage Two*, you roll the ball along the line towards the back of the hole, stopping the swing, as previously, at the outside of the left foot. Do this with all six balls until all have nestled in the cup.

The next step (*Stage Four*) is to apply the right hand to the swing movement we have just learned. When you have done this, you should feel that the right elbow is somewhat bent and that the right arm is giving support to the left, a role it will play in every golf shot you make. The extra strength a right-handed player has in his right arm will always be controlled by the left. The golf swing is a two-sided movement—the left acts while the right reacts.

With both hands now on the putter, repeat the exercises in *Stage Three*. Feel how the left arm leads and the right hand and arm support. Be careful that the stronger right hand and arm do not take

13

The right shoulder sinks but does not move outward. Keep the line across the shoulders parallel with your hips and feet.

STAGE FOUR
Start at the address position with the right arm hanging relaxed.

Allow the right shoulder to drop, until the right hand is opposite a point on the shaft under the left hand.

Still relaxed, move the right hand over and hold the club in exactly the same way as the left hand, with the right thumb on top of the grip.

control. Next, repeat the exercise from a distance of 24 inches from the hole. To do this, you may have to take a longer back-swing. What I don't want you to do is to increase the tempo of your arm-swing.

This should remain constant for a while yet. The following table summarizes the training necessary to stabilize this first part of your swing development.

PRACTICE SESSION NO. 1

Drill	Distance From Hole	Success (Par)	Remarks
1	12''	6	Left hand/arm only
2	12''	6	Both arms – left arm dominating
3	24''	5	Both arms for drives 3 – 6
4	48''	4	The remaining 2 should be within 6'' of the hole
5	72''	2	The remaining 4 should be within 6'' of the hole
6	108''	1	The remaining 5 should be within 10'' of the hole

Your "starter grip"
Move the right hand up until it fits snugly beside the left, forming a unit. This grip will serve during the first two stages of the swing-building process.

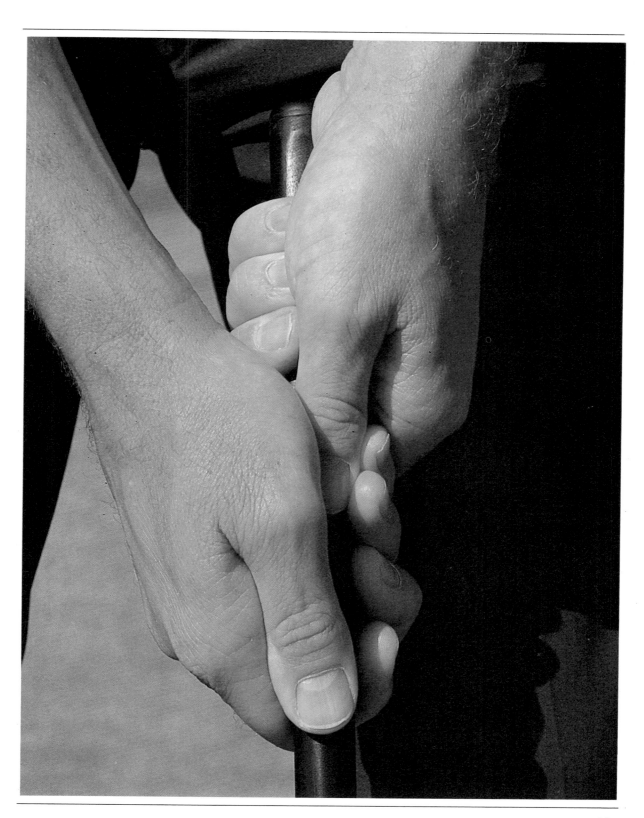

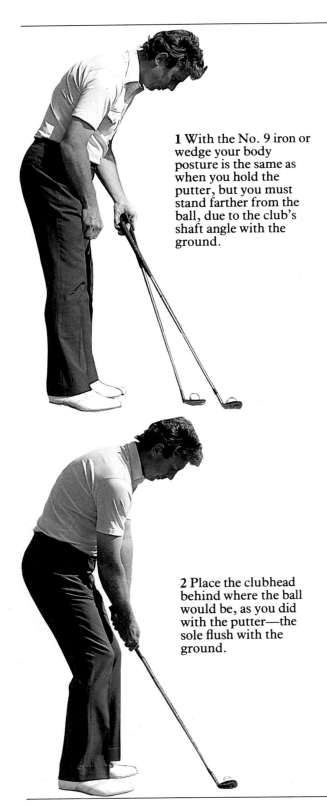

1 With the No. 9 iron or wedge your body posture is the same as when you hold the putter, but you must stand farther from the ball, due to the club's shaft angle with the ground.

3 Hold the club as you did the putter, with the hands together and the thumbs down the top of the grip. You can see that the grip is circular, but keep the putting hand grip all the same. Have the hands slightly more to the left (in line with the eventual ball position) than you had when you were using the putter.

2 Place the clubhead behind where the ball would be, as you did with the putter—the sole flush with the ground.

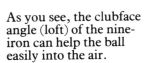

As you see, the clubface angle (loft) of the nine-iron can help the ball easily into the air.

4 Some practice swings now: clubhead back to 6 inches past the right foot, easy grandfather-clock tempo.
5 Then down and brush the grass where the ball will lie, continuing the swing until the 6-inches-past-the-foot position. Remember the golden rule: the left arm is the leading star, the right is the supporting cast.

Do this a few times and then try it with a ball. Don't be tempted to scoop the ball into the air—remember that the club's built-in loft does it for you. You just make the arm/club pendulum movement down and through the ball, and it will pop up like magic. See! Success once again!

STEP TWO: The short swing

The simple pendulum movement that you have mastered is going to be used in the first part of the next stage in your swing-development program, but this time with another club. The putter which you have used so far is the simplest club to use, mainly because of its easy-to-control length. As you see from the club-set diagram on page 32, the next clubs in length and manageability are the three irons: No. 9, No. 10 (the pitching wedge), and sand wedge (also called the sand iron). For this stage, you may use the nine iron or the pitching wedge, whichever you want.

The major difference between these clubs and the putter is in the design of the clubhead. The purpose of the putter is to roll the ball along the ground, while the nine iron and the pitching wedge are meant to help the ball into the air. These clubs, and the sand wedge, fly the ball best into the air. This is mainly due to the angle (also called the "loft") of the clubface. Because of this angle, identical strikes on the ball with a putter and an iron will have

17

Locked hips and legs make it difficult to throw a ball far.

If you can move your hips and legs freely, the ball can be thrown much farther.

completely different results: the putted ball will roll, while the pitched ball will jump up into the air. You don't have to do anything extra or make any special change to your swing movement in order to lift the ball from the ground—*the club does it for you.*

Now try the exercise on the previous page.

Up to now, most of the work done has come from the partnership between the arms/ hands unit and the club. The one-piece, or single-lever, movement has served us well when striking the ball. The loft of the club has caused the ball to lift, and the result has been a rather unspectacular, short lob that flies for a few yards—hardly the image you had of your golf when you first decided to play the game. But be patient, we are now going to liven things up! Gradually, we will expand the pendulum movement and thus the length of the shot. However, let me point out that the single-lever movement is the most controlled swing in your game.

STEP THREE: Making the ball go farther

In order to make the ball go farther, you must create more speed out at the clubhead, without losing the correct contact between the clubface and the ball. In other words, while building up the swing, you must not lose control of the clubhead to the extent that the hit strays away from the sweetspot, or the perfect striking area. (On a well-designed club, the sweetspot is found in the center of the clubface and is the point where the lines of balance meet.)

"The legs and hips are the engine of the swing and the arms and hands are the transmission system." This quotation is from the scientific study referred to in the introduction, and it describes quite well, if broadly, the two working areas into which our swing-building scheme divides. The hands hold the club; the arms work in

Any sort of "throwing" or hitting activity from the hands would not give the desired power out at the end of the string.

Imagine you have a weight on a string. To create speed you must *lead* the weight through a down-ward-pulling movement thst you initiate with the arms.

CORRECT

WRONG

unison with the hands to swing it; and the major power comes from the correct stance and movement of the body. Here is a simple experiment which illustrates this point.

Stand with your feet about 6 inches apart and, without moving your legs or hips, throw a golf ball as far as you can. Now throw another ball, but this time, you move your legs and hips as much as you like, keeping your feet in the same position (your feet are allowed to lift from the ground). You will now have a longer throw, and it will feel much more natural for you to co-ordinate your arm's movements with those of your body. This ball-throwing action is similar in many ways to the golf swing, and I will be using this comparison where necessary during the rest of the swing-development program.

While practicing, get into the rhythm of the swing by using the grandfather-clock method, repeating the words, "back and through" or "one and two" as you swing.

These rhythm phrases can be applied to the arms and knees as well, to assist the co-ordination of movement between the two.

The two-lever movement

You should now be finding that your swing has automatically widened on both sides—back and through—and that you are beginning to feel the movement a little stiff and limiting. It is time to allow the wrists to become active so that the clubhead can begin to move farther back and through in a natural manner. From this point, our golf swing ceases to be a one-lever movement and becomes a two-lever movement. The first lever is the left arm together with the supporting right arm, down to the wrists. The second lever is from the wrists, which function as a hinge, through the hands to the end of the club.

Let's jump ahead and look at this two-lever system in a finished backswing. The hinge, or wrists, require only enough

19

The thumb and first finger "feel" the club. The three other fingers support it.

The two hands come together like two pieces in a jigsaw puzzle.

The Overlapping Grip
With your left hand, hold the club out in front of you.

Place your right hand on the club and slide the hand up the grip until your left thumb is fitting snugly into the center of your right palm.

It is important to fit the hands together at the illustrated points first.

tension to support and control the weight of the club as it moves back to the end of the backswing. Too much tension locks the hinge, too little makes for loose play. This fine balance of tension is created initially in the hands during the address. To accommodate this hinging movement, the hands must work together as a unit, sitting together as snugly as possible. As we do not all have the same size fingers and hands, the grip you have had up to now (the two hands on the club grip, the one close under the other) may not be acceptable. Try the grip shown in the illustrations.

The grip
At first, the grip will feel strange. Later on, it will become natural and comfortable, providing stability without your having to hold the club too hard (which causes unwanted tension in the wrists and through into the arms and shoulders).

The golf grip in which the right hand's little finger overlaps the left hand's index finger is, logically enough, known as the overlapping grip.

If you have large hands or long fingers, you may have to fiddle around to find a position whereby the little finger on the right hand combines both hands, while still giving you the feeling that it is the left hand that is the master, guiding hand.

The two-fisted, or non-overlapping, grip is known as the baseball grip, for obvious reasons.

There is a third grip which should be mentioned, if for no other reason than that it is used by one of the greatest players of all time, Jack Nicklaus. This is the interlocking grip, made by locking the hands together by knotting the left hand's little finger with the right hand's index finger. Players with small hands and short fingers may use this as an alternative to the baseball grip.

The grip plays an important role in the golf swing, because it links the two levers in a fixed, but not locked, fashion. The upper lever (the left arm, with the supporting right arm) is fixed naturally to the shoulders—but as you noticed with the short swing, as soon as you start to swing the left arm back, the left shoulder moves in orbit around the center point of the swing (which is the center point on the upper chest). This point is all-important, because it provides a fixed center-of-operations (if it stays central) for our rotating lever system. Try to keep in

Close your fingers
around the grip. Lift the
little finger of the right
hand off the club.

Slide the right hand
against the left and
lower the little finger
onto the index finger of
the left hand.

Shuffle the hands a little
to find a compact and
comfortable final
position.

mind, especially as your swing grows in pace
and size, that this center point should not be
exposed to too much stress, or else the lever
system will come out of line with the ball.

Look at the illustrations on the next page
and see what we did with the small swing.
The upper lever led the lower lever back
without much bending at the wrists for the
first few inches. Then, as the upper lever

continues to move back, the wrists bend
further, creating the angle between the two
levers.

The half backswing
For the purpose of swing building, we shall
stop halfway up on the backswing with the
left arm about parallel to the ground. Note
that the supporting right arm has tucked in

Those players with
small hands and fingers
will probably be better
off just combining the
two hands as described

above (left thumb in
right hand), leaving all
fingers on the grip. This
is the baseball grip.

The interlocking grip.

Whatever you do, it is
important that the
hands combine to work
and feel as one.

21

Adopt the address position, but without the club. Let your arms hang loosely, and then bring your hands together.

Swing the arms back as before. But this time, let the left knee follow the right, as if it was being drawn by the left arm.

Hold that position! The important thing is the coordination between the left arm and the left knee, which made the right knee move back slightly, creating freedom for the arms.

and that the right shoulder has turned back as a result of the rotating lever system. Be sure that there is just enough tension in the left hand and arm to support the club in this position. The angle between left arm and club (upper and lower levers) varies from player to player but should lie somewhere between 130° and 140°. Remember that this angle returns to about 90° when you are at the top of the backswing. At this halfway back position, you should feel that you start the forward swing by coordinating, as before, the left arm and the left knee—one can almost say the whole left side of the body. Allow the speed out at the end of the lower lever—the clubhead—to build up gradually, due to the pulling-down-and-through action of the upper lever—the left arm and the supporting right arm. Keep a low arm-speed in order to be able to influence, feel, and check where you have your swing. Don't think about the length of your shots—that is further down the road as yet.

Now swing forward, keeping the left-arm/left-knee coordination.	Through where the ball would lie.	And stop. The movement has taken your right knee with it.

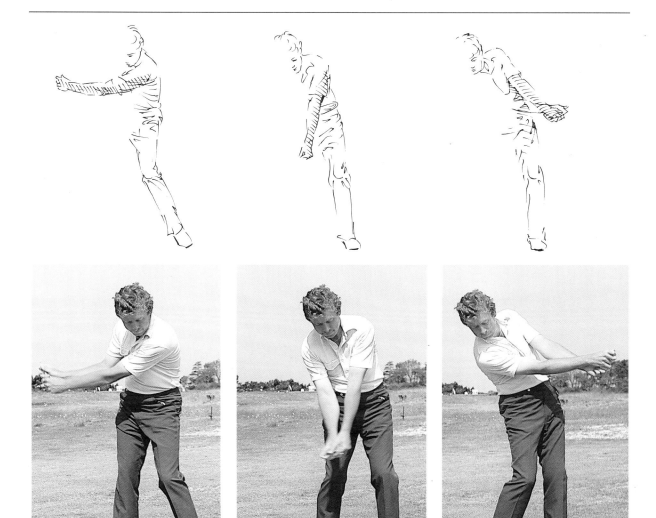

Another point in this backswing position is that of the clubhead. During the backswing, the left arm has rotated itself and the clubhead so that the face of the club is almost directly away from you.

Now try to experience the force that builds up as you *lead* the club down and through. "Feel the force, don't force the feel!" Allow the clubhead to overtake the arms after impact, rotating the arms to approximately a mirror reflection of the backswing stop position on what is termed the follow-through side of the swing. Note that the right knee has been "pulled" through and the right foot has rolled on the inside, finishing up balanced on the forward half, with the heel off the ground.

Take a few practice swings through the spot where the ball will lie, brushing the grass so that the clubhead will come under the ball and thereby lift it. Again, don't be tempted to scoop the ball—swing *down* and the ball will lift *up*.

Now, with the ball on a tee (half an inch

23

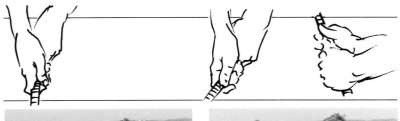

Now take the nine iron or the pitching wedge and swing it through the ball, first placing it on a tee, about half an inch above the ground. An easy way to measure is to tee up the ball using the thickness of your fingers as a guide.

In this first phase of expanding your golf swing, the left arm pulls the left knee with it on the backswing and the right knee with it on the forward swing. The swing's engine may be in the legs and hips, but the ignition key is the knees.

From this stage until the full swing is in place, the ball will be struck from the teed position. This allows margin for error and helps us to succeed more often during the sensitive swing-building process.

up), play some shots, occasionally stopping to check the backswing and the follow-through finishing positions. Be sure your swing is easy and rhythmic. Now I realize that, in the short space of time that the swing takes, you cannot think of many things—one key thought is probably all that you can manage. The ultimate aim of your training, therefore, is to have a programmed movement which is triggered by feelings of rhythm and pace.

Before we progress further, it is time to say something about practice. Practice is something that you do either to improve or maintain a level of skill that you have reached. Sometimes, in order to progress, you must go back a stage or two in order to find the

confidence needed to prepare yourself for the next stage. A practice session that has as its goal a "next step" in development should start at least one rung below in order to reinforce that which has already been learned. Therefore, I would suggest that your practice at this point should start on the putting green where you began and continue to the practice area, where you should work on the short swing, using a nine iron or a pitching wedge. "Success" with the short swing means lifting the ball into the air a minimum of eight times out of ten over three series of ten shots. Only after this should you move on to the half swing. Success here should be a minimum of seven shots out of ten, again over three series of ten shots.

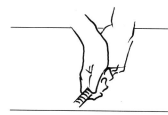 

Stay and practice any step that you are not happy with. Never be too proud to go back a stage and build up.

A practice session can look like the table on the right.

PRACTICE SESSION NO. 2

Step	Drill	Success (Par)
1	Putting with 6 balls 24'' from hole	Average 5 in a hole – 3 series
2	Putting with 6 balls 72'' from hole	Average 2 in a hole, 3 series: remainder maximum 6'' away
3	Short swing with iron (wedge), 10 balls	Average 8 shots up in the air – 3 series
4	Half swing with iron (wedge), 10 balls	Average 7 shots up in the air – 3 series

STEP FOUR: The full swing

You will have noticed that, so far, our only ambition has been to strike the ball correctly and frequently, without great expectations as regards accuracy or length. These qualities can be looked for when our full swing has developed into a stable shot.

To my way of thinking, the swing must be programmed to such an extent that the face of the clubhead (on all the clubs) can find the back of the ball just about all the time. Then we can turn our attention to the controlled flight of our shots. Don't think of hitting the ball a long way until your striking consistency is at the success level indicated in the two practice tables (*pages 14 and above*).

"Oh dear", I can hear you say. "I'll never get out on a golf course." You will—and sooner than you think—if you stick to the program and try not to be impatient. The final step in the swing development program is to complete the backswing and to balance it with a finished follow-through.

A larger swing demands a sound base, so you must make two changes in your address position. The first change is to widen your stance so that the distance between your feet is about 24 inches, or a little less if you are below average height. Should you make the stance too wide, the natural turning-back-and-through movement will be restricted. Too narrow a stance will give you poor balance.

Using a nine iron or a pitching wedge, and with the ball on its tee as usual, adopt the address position for the full swing, with about 24 inches between your feet. "Sit" a little more, using your behind to achieve a nice, balanced stance.

Swing slowly back.

1

2

The second change in your address position is, to put it bluntly, that you must stick your behind out as if you were going to sit at a bar stool. Tension in the lower back will result, and this, together with the widened stance, should create a more stable feeling from the hips down. Don't lock the lower half of the body too much. Your feeling should be one of balance, with the body weight towards the toes and the knees flexed slightly. As before, the upper body bends from the hips forward, with the arms hanging naturally and the shoulders relaxed, ready to be rotated by the arm swing.

Important checkpoints are:
1. Between 70 and 80 per cent of the total body weight should be over a firmly braced right leg.
2. The left knee should point to the right of the ball.

(One of the myths of the golf swing is that the left foot must remain firmly on the ground throughout the swing, but if, in order to attain the full, turned-shoulder position, you feel that it is necessary to let the left heel come up, then do so.)

The most important aim of the backswing

. . . round. . .

5

. . .until the left shoulder has almost tucked itself under your chin. The hinge at the wrists has continued to bend gradually inwards (towards you), until it comes to its natural physical stop, creating an angle of about 90° between the arms and the club. The club is now "parked" at the end of the backswing (or the beginning of the for- ward swing). This position will vary from player to player, depending on build, strength, and flexibility.

Right arm folding in at the elbow, shoulders turned back by arms.

Stop at the halfway position. Be sure that the stance is the same as that practiced earlier, and that there is no tension in the right arm/shoulder area.

If all is well, allow the left arm to continue its journey. . .

3

4

is to reach a position from which the forward swing will be effective. Remember the ball-throwing test we did earlier? In order to generate more power, you had to use your hips and legs. Now feel the same movement as you start to swing forward. Don't do anything consciously with the lever system, just experience how the left knee/hip drives sideways. Stop and feel the tension that is building up between the upper and lower body, with the lower half activated while the upper half waits, storing power that is to be unleashed through the lever system and will produce a reaction out in the clubhead,

releasing the stored-up power through the ball in a whiplash effect.

Swing back and start the downswing again; stop once more and feel the tension build up. Repeat several times, so that you get things in the right order. This is the decisive part of the swing and getting it all in the right order means that your "swing timing" is correct.

After the leg/hip start to the downswing, you will notice your body's lever system moving down a little towards what is termed the "pocket area", around the right hip and pocket. This position can only be attained if

However, the left arm should finish within the sector shown in the illustration. If this is not the case, alter the track that the arm has followed during the backswing, until the arm arrives comfortably in that sector.

Hips have moved sideways somewhat, shoulders and arms following.

6

The power is released, almost back to the address position with the arms and club.

Through the ball . . . The arms rotate in a "scissors" fashion.

7

8

the right hand/arm unit has kept its supporting role and has not tried to break out on its own. From this pocket area, the clubhead can move to the ball along the correct approach lane, giving the maximum power release (like an uppercut in boxing), as well as a secure feeling of arms/body coordination. From here on in, the swing is released and the reaction through the ball occurs. The energy that you have created and stored is released via the lever system, rotating the arms and clubhead to square at impact, and the arms continue to swing further through. The left side of the body, which initiated the forward swing, turned out of the way and left room for the arms to move freely and for the right side to extend towards the target and to move on to a balanced finishing position.

Right heel off the ground, right side moving through, past the left.

The hips are now facing the target, and the shoulders are being rotated a little more by the arms and club.

9

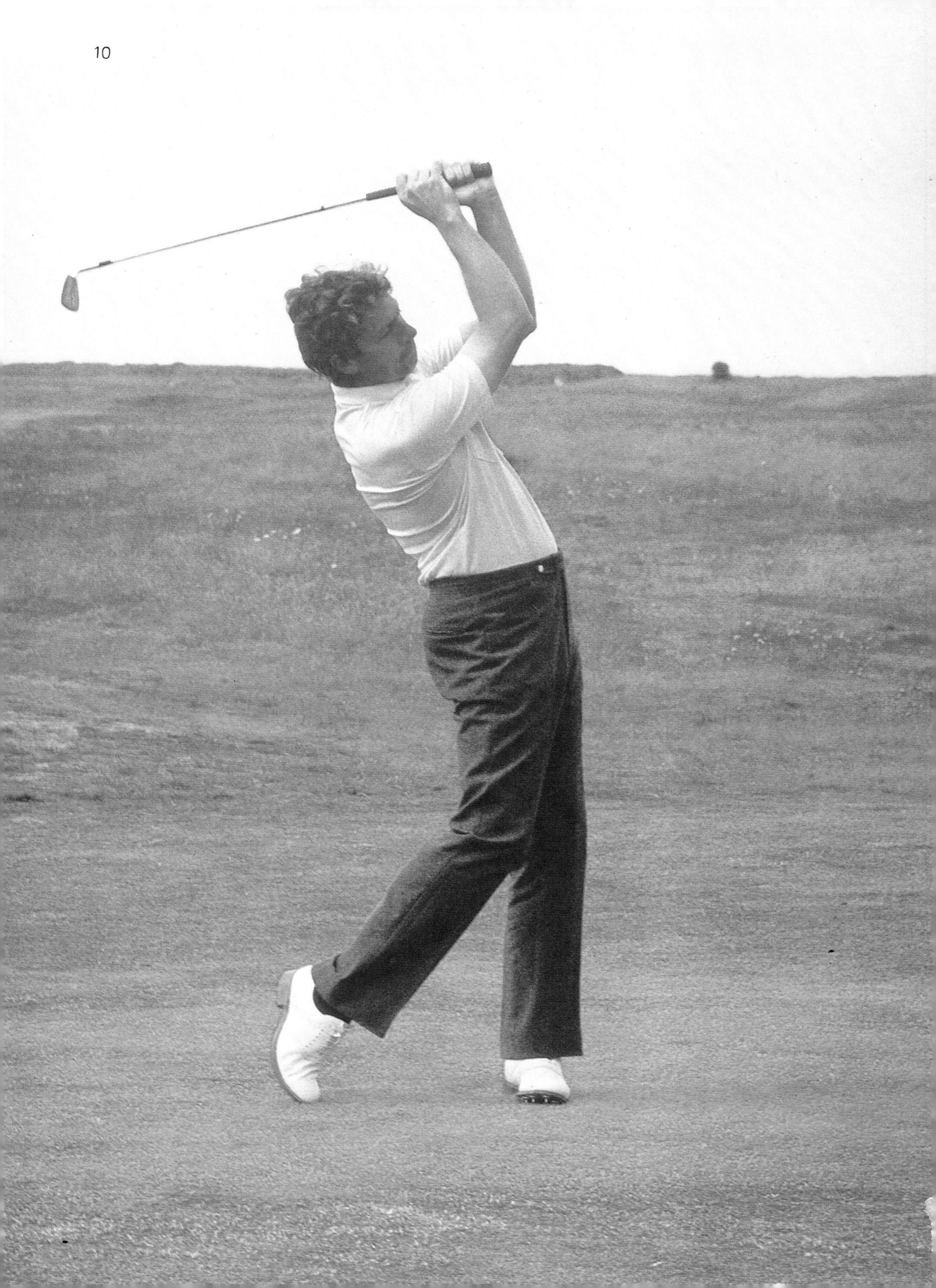

Although the swing has been built up in stages, the aim is to have a *total* feeling for the movement.

Rhythm is important. Find your own key; it can be, for example, "back and through" or "one and two".

The word "and" can be the pause between back and forward swing.

Now that we have arrived at the final stage of our swing construction, I would like your mental picture of your swing to be based on the following:
1. A stable, easy and alert address position: Position 1.
2. A balanced, controlled end-of-back-swing/start-of-forward-swing position: Position 2.
3. An end-of-swing-position to which the arms have led the club in a free towards-the-target movement: Position 3.

4. These three positions are controlled by the center point in the upper chest. The all-important impact position is not experienced while you hit the ball. It is simply a result of the swing movements and the positions which precede it.

The golf swing and the wooden club

At this point, we should try to define the "creature" which we call the golf swing. It is the movement that the body makes together with different golf clubs to produce an assortment of shots. We have a maximum of around 14 clubs to help us on the course, and these—when married to our swing—cover most of the situations we are liable to find on the course.

Many such situations will be gone through in this book, with discussion of the eventual adjustments we make to the basic golf swing that we have built up. The most common variation on the theme occurs when we select one of the wooden clubs. By the time you read this, you will probably have tried to hit some shots with a wooden club, and experienced changes in your concept and feeling of the golf swing. Apart from the distinctive shape of the clubhead, the most noticeable difference is the feeling of swinging a longer club. It's like switching from driving a small compact sedan to a large station-wagon. You know how to control it, but you need a while to get to know where you've got it.

Wooden clubs are available with lofts that increase by about 3° from No. 1 through

No. 7. A standard set consists of Nos. 1, 3, 4, and 5. The No. 7 wood (called a ginty) is a utility club for special lies that is becoming more and more popular as a replacement for a No. 5 iron. The No. 6 wood has to be special-ordered. The two main swing-influencing differences between the woods and irons, in a standard golf set, are loft, shaft length, and distance. The former is less obvious than the latter.

The standard loft of a No. 1 wood (driver) is about 11°–12°, and that of a No. 5 wood is about 21°–22° which is the same as for a No. 2 iron. This doesn't mean that the five-wood and the two-iron produce the same shot. The five-wood shaft is longer, by about 3–4 inches, and has more mass centralized behind the club blade's sweetspot, thereby creating more power for height and length of the shot.

Swing technique adjustments

The length of shaft differences between irons and woods create different clubhead arc shapes (*page 33*). For instance, the clubhead arc with the No. 9 iron, 34 inches long, will be shorter and more steeply descending into the ball-striking area than, say, the No. 1 wood of 42 inches length. The head design on the iron is made for slight downswing strokes. But the flatter-soled wood likes to

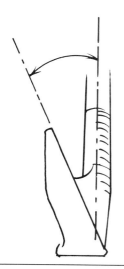

On an iron club, loft is defined as the angle of the face to the center line of the shaft. On a wood, it is the angle of the face to a line perpendicular to the sole of the wood.

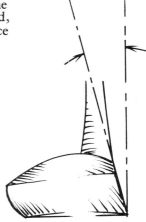

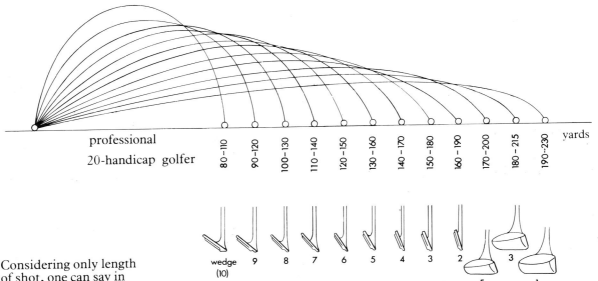

professional

20-handicap golfer

| | 80-110 | 90-120 | 100-130 | 110-140 | 120-150 | 130-160 | 140-170 | 150-180 | 160-190 | 170-200 | 180-215 | 190-230 | yards |

| wedge (10) | 9 | 8 | 7 | 6 | 5 | 4 | 3 | 2 | 3 | | |
| | | | | | | | | | 5 | 1 | |

Considering only length of shot, one can say in general that the No. 2 iron is next in line after the No. 5 wood for a top player.

sweep over the grass in a landing-aircraft type of approach to the ball, striking it at the bottom of the swing arc when being played directly from the grass, and slightly after this point—on the upswing—when from a tee.

Where is the bottom of the arc? you may ask. Well, this can vary from player to player. Test it by swinging with a wood and noting where the clubhead contacts the grass for the most part. This will probably be somewhere opposite your outer left shoulder. Play some shots from a tee pegged about 1.5 inches over ground level. If you are hitting a mixture of topped and "skied" (high, short) shots, you probably have the ball positioned too far to the right. Topped or thinned low shots give an indication of balls teed too far to the left.

When playing directly from the grass with a No. 3 or 5 wood, stand with the ball more to the right—by one ball's width—than the established teed-up ball position. With wood shots, also note:

(a) Too fast backswings build up an uncontrollable amount of needless power on the backswing. *Place* the club in position at the start of the forward swing.

(b) You have an increased general swing tempo. Remember that the longer shaft will create a higher clubhead speed—you don't need to swing your arms or move your body faster.

(c) Although it may not look like it, there is a fair amount of loft on the wooden clubs—enough to lift the ball provided the clubface is correctly presented to the ball.

(d) Off-center hits lose length. Controlled striking means maximum potential shot distance.

In other words, give the woods a chance to show what they can do for you, without altering your standard golf swing movement. Work towards a feeling that you and your muscles are doing 30% of the job, and your swing and club the remaining 70%.

Summary
A build-up program has now been presented, from the initial pendulum swing with the putter and with the lofted club, through the two-lever half-swing back and through, to the "three-position" full swing around the center point.

I started this book by saying that there *is* no model swing, and I do not wish to now steer you into a movement which you will find unnatural. The medium of the written word is by no means a substitute for the one-to-one instruction that you can get from

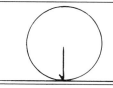

These two drawings give a general picture of the difference in clubhead arc between a short iron (for instance, a No. 9) and a wooden club.

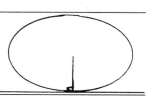

a qualified golf teacher. But what I have attempted in this chapter, and indeed throughout the book, is to suggest an individual swing-development program that can function as a guide for everyone and as a complement to "live" professional instruction. You only need to study the swing-sequence pictures of successful players to see that no two swings are alike, even if all functioning swings have certain fundamental elements in common. It is on these fundamentals that I have based the program.

Practice

The further you go in the development program, the more the responsibility for your progress shifts to you. The major part of your progress relies on the quantity and quality of your practice sessions.

The putting-green stage can now become more of a preparation in rhythm and a reminder that the left arm must dominate the swing.

The half-swing is an important stage, as this has all the ingredients of the full swing in a scaled-down form and, therefore, is easier to work with and test. It is with this swing that your range practice can start, still with the ball on the tee.

When you feel confident with your ball striking, progress to the full swing, still with an easy tempo. Start to think of a track which the left arm follows, back to position 2 and then down through the pocket area, past impact, and through to the finished-swing position 3. This left-arm track connects the three swing positions, and is often referred to as the "plane" of the swing. The track which the clubhead follows back and through is called the "path" of the swing.

Remember while practicing at this stage that it is the swing programming and control, with the resultant consistency in ball striking, that is your goal. For the moment, ignore the fact that your shots may fly to the left or right, or not far enough, as we will cover this subject in the next chapter. But when we get to that stage, we should be

PRACTICE SESSION No. 3

Drill	Purpose	Success (Par)
Putting Green 6 putts from 3ft 6 putts from 10ft 6 putts from 20ft	Getting started; feeling club – left arm dominating.	No specific goals; relaxed, positive start to session.
Practice Area 10 balls on tee with No. 9/ wedge using a half swing.	Still building up feelings, rhythm; feel club working.	Allow club to work for you. Five good shots.
10 balls on tee with No. 9/ wedge using half swing. Repeat.	More concen-trated practice. Allow lever sys-tem to function.	8 good shots of each series of 10.
10 balls on tee with No. 9 iron/ wedge using full swing.	Feel power build up in back-swing. Check position 2, feel left arm in plane.	No specific goals because of swing checks.
10 balls on tee with No. 9 iron/ wedge using full swing.	More concen-trated practice, feel total rhythm in swing.	7 good shots of 10.
As previous drill using No. 7 or 8 iron. Repeat.	Begin to feel same swing with longer club, keep tempo; note shot length increase.	No goal in first series. Second series: 7 good shots of 10.

Approximately 75 practice balls required.
Length of time for practice session approximately 50 minutes.

confident that with the full swing at an easy tempo we can hit seven out of ten shots from a wooden tee by using a lofted club.

Chapter 2
UNDERSTANDING BALL FLIGHT PRINCIPLES

The full swing movement you built up in the first chapter will, with practice, provide you with an approximate 70 per cent striking success. As a high-handicap golfer, your accuracy will vary, as you are not going to be able to strike the ball with the sweetspot every time. You may manage it two, three, or perhaps four times in a row with a full swing during a practice session, but that is probably as often as you can expect during the initial development period.

Top professionals such as Jack Nicklaus and Tom Watson have got the swing down to a fine art, and yet even they can have several imperfect strikes per round of golf. Certainly their mistakes in striking are not as great as the average golfer's, but things would be different if they had as little control over the power generated in their swings as many "weekend" players have. The biggest trap that a learning golfer can fall into is trying to hit the ball far without having sufficient swing control. Many high-handicap players remain just that more because of this fault than any other, and it is my belief that the careers of many talented youngsters have stagnated as a result of their eagerness for length at too early a stage of development.

Golf is essentially a game of control. A survey of the top money-winners playing the tour in the United States shows few winners of long-driving competitions. On the other hand, the pros who find a lot of fairway grass from the tee and can reach the greens in regulation (first shot on par 3 holes, second on par 4 holes, third on par 5 holes) have usually banked a fair amount of cash.

So concentrate your early practice sessions upon controlling your golf swing, in order to be able to present the hitting area (clubface) of the clubhead correctly to the ball at the moment of impact. This chapter is concerned with what happens at that crucial moment.

The flight characteristics of our shots are governed by five indisputable factors, referred to as "the ball-flight laws". All of these influence the clubhead's arrival at the ball, and therefore the resultant golf shot. If all five factors are "obeyed" at impact, we have achieved a perfect striking position and, all other things being equal, the grand golf shot.

Moreover, if you understand these factors, you will have a good grasp of the workings of your golf swing, and this will make your practice sessions more interesting and productive. We will deal with them, not in any order of importance, but rather as I feel they should be built into your golf swing.

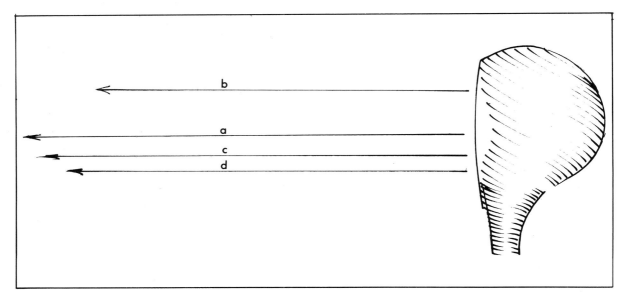

Tests made by the G.S.G.B. research team mentioned in the introduction show how much distance is lost by a golfer when he does not hit the ball with the sweetspot.

(*a*) With the sweetspot.
(*b*) ¾ inch from the sweetspot.
(*c*) ¼ inch from the sweetspot.
(*d*) ½ inch from the sweetspot.

1. Where on the blade the ball is struck

The first factor is easy, as we have already experienced the importance of the perfect striking point in the clubface, the sweetspot. Contact anywhere else means loss of length, and often of control, in your shots. The design of the clubhead can, to some degree, compensate for the negative effects of "non-center" hits. An iron club or metal wood designed with so-called heel/toe weighting can extend the size of the sweetspot in the direction of the clubhead's heel or toe. Similarly, a club that has more head weight situated lower down, towards the sole of the head, can help stabilize strikes below the sweetspot.

The training sessions of the first chapter contain the keys to accurate striking. Be realistic when you begin a practice session, don't start with a full swing—start on the putting green and build up towards the full swing. Don't leave one level until the previous "success level" of competence has been attained. Remember that even if everything else at impact is correct, the shot will not be exactly as you had planned, if you do not hit the ball with the sweetspot.

2. How the clubhead approaches the ball

On the backswing, the clubhead moves back and up into the air. On the forward swing, it moves down and returns to the original starting, or address, position. The steepness or shallowness of the forward-swing path, by which the clubhead approaches the ball, is the subject of our second law of flight.

If the approach is perfect, impact with the irons will be slightly before the bottom of the arc made by the clubhead, and a little later with the wooden clubs, at which point the wooden club's head will be parallel to the ground. This means that the ball will be struck with the chosen club's loft. If the angle of approach is too steep, the effective loft at impact will be reduced, causing the ball to fly lower than planned, or with an extremely steep downswing, the ball may not fly at all—it may just roll along the ground, since the contact point between club and ball is too high up on the ball (above its center of gravity) and too low on the clubface.

One of the main reasons that a golfer with a reasonably correct golf swing tops a shot in

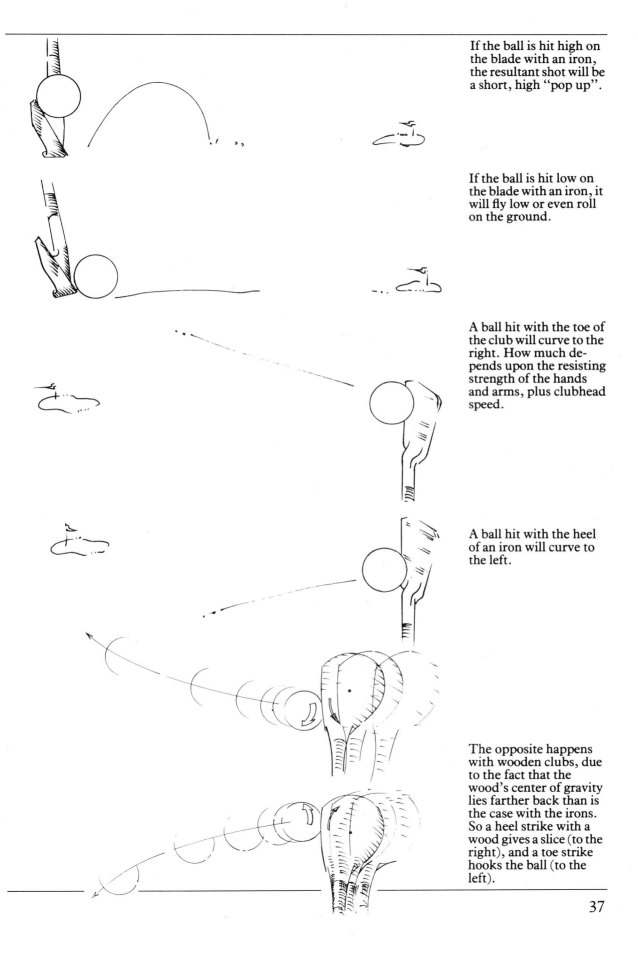

If the ball is hit high on the blade with an iron, the resultant shot will be a short, high "pop up".

If the ball is hit low on the blade with an iron, it will fly low or even roll on the ground.

A ball hit with the toe of the club will curve to the right. How much depends upon the resisting strength of the hands and arms, plus clubhead speed.

A ball hit with the heel of an iron will curve to the left.

The opposite happens with wooden clubs, due to the fact that the wood's center of gravity lies farther back than is the case with the irons. So a heel strike with a wood gives a slice (to the right), and a toe strike hooks the ball (to the left).

perfect	early	late

The perfect angle of approach between the clubhead path and the ground results in a strike at the bottom of the arc, with the clubhead parallel to the ground.

If the clubhead strikes the ball too early in the downswing, the shot will be topped.

If the ball is struck late, the shot will be thinned, as the swing-control center point will be too far forward at impact.

Mis-hit: the club face meets the ball too late because the player tries to scoop it into the air.

Mis-hit: the club face meets the ball too early due to the effort to put too much power into the swing.

this way is, once again, the urge to make longer shots. If you try to force more power into the shot, you can, without being aware of it, easily move your body forward (towards the target). This in effect shifts the swing-control center point (*see page 30*) and puts the swing out of line with the ball—too far forward. The effect is the same as if you had the ball too far back (to your right) at address. This means that the clubhead does not have time to flatten out in its arc and to come down low enough to strike the back of the ball. In other words, the clubhead is still too much in the steeper part of the forward swing when it comes into contact with the ball, and it hits the ball too early.

If the ball was sitting on a wooden tee, the clubhead that approaches too steeply would go directly under the ball, creating a strike high on the clubface above the sweetspot, giving a short, high "pop-up" shot. This type of shot, with one of the wood clubs, would almost certainly leave a mark (often the color of the ball) on the top front edge of the head. So the angle of approach is often one of the more influential factors that lie behind strikes which are high or low on the clubface.

Another mis-hit caused by the wrong angle of approach occurs when you hit the ball too late, that is, *after* the low point of the arc of the clubhead path. This strike is made low (under the sweetspot) on the clubface, and results in shorter, lower than normal, ball flight. We often refer to this type of shot as a "thin" shot, if not soundly struck. In extreme cases, the ball is "topped", as the clubhead has come up from the perfect hit position so that the lower part of the clubface contacts the back of the ball. This kind of topped shot is often due to the player trying to lift or scoop the ball into the air, instead of allowing the loft of the clubhead to do the job.

To summarize, we can say that the angle of clubhead approach influences whether

The impossible ideal. If the golf club could be swung so that its path around the swing-control center was like that of a ferris-wheel around its axle while the wheel rotated in the direction of the target, you would have the perfect swing path.

The paths followed by the driver (a), the No. 5 iron (b), and the No. 9 iron (c) are compared here to the ferris-wheel path (d).

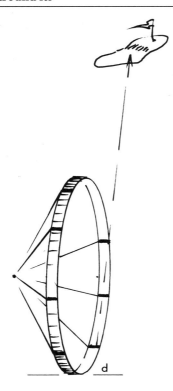

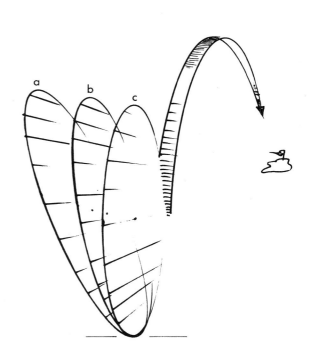

the strike will be high, centered, or low on the club blade and ball, and consequently, the trajectory and length of the ball flight.

3. The clubhead's path direction at impact

The track followed by the clubhead, back and through the golf swing, is referred to as the path. (Actually the clubhead has two paths, one back and one forward, but they can feel like the same path during the swing.) The ideal swing path is one that is always on line to the target and resembles a ferris wheel. Unfortunately, this is a physical impossibility for the golfer, who is standing not upon the line to the target but at one side of it.

When you use a putter, you stand as close to the line between ball and target as you do at any time in golf. This is due to the putter's short length, and to the angle which the shaft makes with the ground when the sole of the clubhead is correctly positioned—an angle referred to as the club's "lie". When you use a longer club, you automatically stand farther from the target line. The longer the club is, the more the built-in lie angle of the club flattens (becomes less upright), and the farther you stand from the target line, until you reach the club that is longest and has the flattest lie—the driver. But the farther you stand from the target line, the flatter and more carousel-like the path that the clubhead follows will become, and the shorter is the stretch of the path over which the clubhead nearly follows the target line.

So remember that it is unnatural to try to force the clubhead back and forward along the line to the target in ferris-wheel fashion. I believe that many golfers have got stuck in their swing development because of this misconception of the golf swing. The longer the club is, the sooner the clubhead leaves the target line, both at the start of the back-

target line outside

inside

a

b

c

Of all the clubs, it is the putter whose path *(a)* keeps closest to the target line. *(b)* The path of the No. 5 iron. *(c)* The path of the driver.

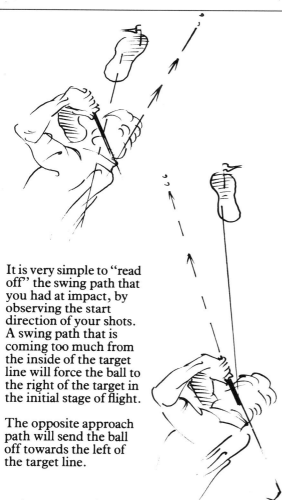

It is very simple to "read off" the swing path that you had at impact, by observing the start direction of your shots. A swing path that is coming too much from the inside of the target line will force the ball to the right of the target in the initial stage of flight.

The opposite approach path will send the ball off towards the left of the target line.

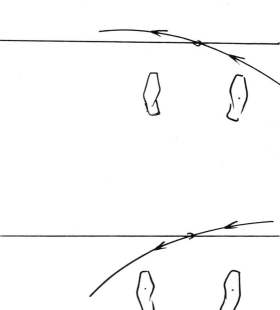

swing and after striking the ball on the forward swing. Interestingly, the average golfer who builds up a clubhead speed of about 100 miles per hour with a driver will create contact between the clubface and ball for only about half a millisecond, through a distance of just ¾ inch! If we consider that all our shots are determined over such a tiny portion of our swing path, then it may be easier to allow the clubhead to leave the path freely on the backswing and the follow-through.

The target line is, as mentioned, the line that runs back from the target through the ball. This is an important reference line which is used quite often when describing the clubhead path of any particular shot. The golf swing doesn't follow the target line, but moves *inside* on the backswing and, on the all-important forward swing, moves from the inside to the line itself at impact, then moves off to the inside of the line again as we continue to the follow-through position. Therefore, the clubhead is *never* on the outside of the target line for a *normal* golf shot.

If, for some reason, this doesn't happen, there are two alternatives. The path of the clubhead will be either too much from the inside, continuing to the outside, or vice versa, from the outside to the inside.

The latter path, from outside to inside, is definitely the most common swing path among average golfers. This path is the basis of golf's best-known shot: the slice; more about this shot later on.

In sum, the swing path at impact decides to a high degree the initial direction of your shots, due to the speed of the clubhead forcing the ball forward along the same path.

41

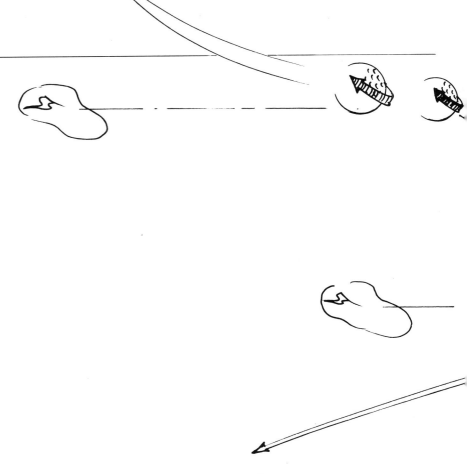

With the blade at impact pointing to the right of our target line (open-face position), the ball is given a sidespin (in this case left-to-right, or clockwise as seen from above), making it curve to the right of the target line—by an amount that depends, of course, on how many degrees the clubface was open. The shot will be shorter than normal, firstly because of the curvature of the shot, since too much power goes into moving the ball sideways instead of forward. Secondly, when the club blade is opened, it is therefore also more lofted, creating a higher-than-normal ball trajectory, so that the ball stops rolling sooner and the shot is shorter.

4. The clubface's impact angle relative to the swing path

We now come to the most crucial factor influencing the direction of the golf shot. We have already looked at one form of club-blade position when we talked about off-center striking and its effect on the length and accuracy of shots *(pages 36 – 37)*. Control over the clubface, of course, is really what the game is all about. There are millions of golfers who can eventually hit the ball as far as most professional players. But a very small percentage of them have the ability to control the clubface position at impact with enough consistency to have the chance of scoring like a pro. In all games which use a club, racquet, or bat to strike a ball, it is control over the connection between the two elements that is paramount. The *angle* of the club blade at impact is important for obtaining both length and accuracy in our shots. What concerns us

here is the blade angle in relation to the swing path.

The perfect impact situation for *accurate* golf shots is when (*a*) the ball is being struck on the sweetspot, the center of the clubface; (*b*) the clubhead is travelling along the path towards the target; and (*c*) the clubface is square to the swing path. Nothing else is needed. Assuming that (*a*) and (*b*) are correct, let's look at what happens if the clubface is wrongly angled.

In both of the illustrated situations, the swing path is perfectly positioned at impact. This means that both shots will start off in the direction of the target—along our target line. But it is the clubface position at impact that is the dominating feature if the blade is open or closed by several degrees. Thus, the shot's initial flight direction will tend towards the direction that the blade is pointing in, and increasingly so as the blade's angle of error increases. Once again,

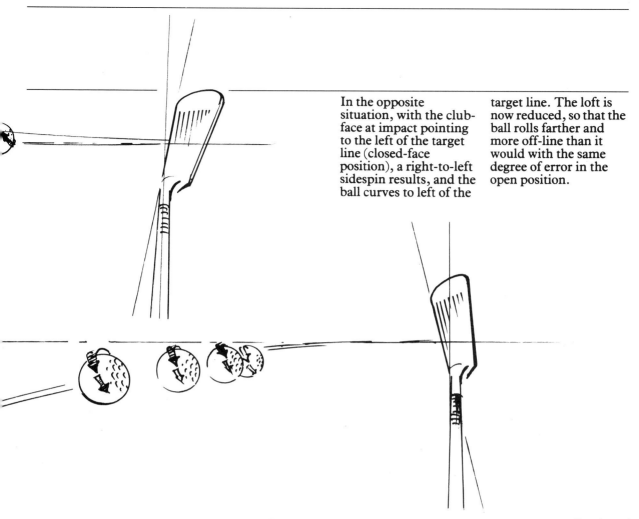

In the opposite situation, with the club-face at impact pointing to the left of the target line (closed-face position), a right-to-left sidespin results, and the ball curves to left of the target line. The loft is now reduced, so that the ball rolls farther and more off-line than it would with the same degree of error in the open position.

this emphasizes the importance of striving after as much control of the club blade as possible.

An interesting illustration is that a mere two degrees of misalignment of the driver clubface at impact will put enough right or left spin on the ball to push it at least 20 yards off the target line—probably into the rough!

5. The clubhead's speed at impact

I have purposely left this factor until the end, not because it is the least significant one, but to stress the fact that your desire for power and length should be curbed until you have attained a fair knowledge of—and level of skill in controlling—the golf swing.

The faster the clubhead is travelling when it contacts the ball, the farther the ball will travel, *providing that the other four factors controlling the ball's flight are fulfilled.* For example, you can achieve a professional level of clubhead speed but, if the clubface is open or closed, you will lose length in relation to a shot that goes *straight* to the target. Or if your control over the clubhead is so erratic that your ball/clubface accuracy varies, then you will never be able to rely upon the length of your shots to the green— some will be too long, others too short, and few will have the right length.

I know it's fun to try and hit a long golf shot, especially from the tee, and far be it from me to deny you that pleasure. All I want you to be able to do is find the ball after you've hit it!

Well, those were the fundamentals influencing the two ingredients of ball flight— direction and length. With this knowledge, you are better equipped to help yourself develop during your practice sessions. Let's now go through such a session, examining some of the routines, ball flights (and non-

Start your line-up routine 4 or 5 yards behind the ball (*a*). Let your eyes trace an imaginary line from the target back through the ball and *vice versa*, until the line is established in your mind. If the target is more than just a few yards away from the ball, as it usually is, then you must create an intermediary "target"—a substitute—which lies on the target line in front of the ball, say at a maximum distance of 4 ft. This is done from the behind-the-ball position. The substitute target (*b*) can be a mark on the ground, a piece of dirt, discolored grass, a broken tee, or anything else that is not likely to move and can be seen easily when you address the ball. (Note that golf rules do not allow you to place anything on the ground that will help with the shot in any way). If there is nothing directly on the line, use something lying to the side as a reference: for example, "my substitute target is three inches to the left of that worm cast".

You have now reduced your target line to about a yard so that it lies directly in front of you when you address the ball.

flights), drills, key thoughts and feelings, which can be useful for your swing development and correction.

Line-up routine

While discussing the laws of ball flight, we noted the importance of the ball-to-target line as a reference. This line is not easy to identify when we stand in the address position, i.e., to one side of the target line. Sighting along the line would then be like trying to aim a rifle with our eyes at the side of the gun-barrel. In order to recognize the line, we must be in a position where we have our eyes along the line and can see the ball aligned with the target: in other words, behind the ball. We show here how you can establish your target line.

Once you are lined up to the ball correctly, and the ball is lined up on the target, a correct swing will make the ball find the target. Later on in your development, it can be interesting to experiment with different stances, more to the left (open) or right (closed), and to observe the effects on your shots. But these are generally used to compensate for a fault or weakness.

After you have come through this line-up routine, it is important for you to know how it *feels* when you are lined up correctly: that is the last step in the sequence. With your body positioned to the target line, move your eyes from the ball along the target line, through the substitute "target", and continuing along that line until you see the actual target. It is imperative that you turn only your head, since a turn of your shoulders alters the line-up position of your body. Notice how it feels when you are lined up properly and are looking at the target. You may feel as though you are aiming left, especially if the target is not many yards away. This is due to the fact that your eyes are sighting along a line which is somewhat to the left of the target line. But don't forget that it is the ball, not you, which is going to the target, and don't change your position—otherwise you may hinder your swing movement.

Last word on lining-up
It is my experience, and presumably that of most teachers of golf, that very often a badly functioning golf swing stems from a faulty line-up position. A fault at set-up is the first

b ⋅————————— a ⋅– – –

⋅————————— ⋅P – – – – – – – – –

⊐ D

The next step is to come around from behind the ball, and place the clubhead at right angles to the line to the intermediary target. Place the clubface behind the ball, using its bottom front edge if an iron, and its top front edge if a wood. Without changing the position of club or arms, take up your address position, with all lines—across your toes, knees, hips and, most importantly, shoulders—*parallel* to the target line in front of you. Thus you are standing in a neutral starting position, from which you can swing freely back and through.

How to check your line-up position. It is a good idea to check that your line-up routine puts you into the correct neutral starting position, as follows. Go through the routine, to the address position. Then, making sure your shoulders are still, lift up the club and hold it about waist-high in front of you, and parallel to the line between the ball and the intermediary "target". From this position, you have a visual check that your body lines (feet, knees, hips, and shoulders) are parallel to the club and, therefore, to the target line.

Turn only your head when you let your eyes run from the ball along the target line, through the intermediate target to the final target. If you turn your shoulders, you will automatically alter the line-up of your body.

Because the line from your eyes to the target is to the left of the target line, you may feel that you are aiming to the left of the target.

link in a chain of compensations that cannot allow the golfer to develop a natural swing. So be careful with that first position—give it the few extra seconds that the line-up routine takes.

Different results with different clubs

As you practice, you will of course obtain different results with different clubs. One main difference is how much the ball curves in flight. For instance, a ball struck with, say, a No. 7 iron that, at impact, happens to have a 3° open clubface (to the right) will not curve the ball as much to the right as does the same clubface fault with a No. 3 wood. This can lead you to believe that the woods are more difficult to use than the irons, and that there must be some extra technique involved in controlling the longer clubs.

Naturally the wooden club, being longer, is a little harder to control. But why is the slice so much greater with the wood than with the iron, despite the same clubface position at impact? When we strike a golf ball with a lofted club, *backspin* is created. The greater the club's loft, the earlier and faster the ball rotates backwards, and this spin makes the ball lift. (Indeed, the only golf shot that is produced without backspin is the putt, which does not lift. It may skid in the very early part of its journey, yet no backspin will occur as long as it is struck with the clubface in the perpendicular position, a zero-degree loft.) If we strike a ball with the clubface's horizontal angle other than square (at 90° to the swing path of the clubhead), *sidespin* is also created. With a lofted club, the No. 7 iron mentioned above, the backspin will dominate over the sidespin. In the case of the No. 3 wood, which has decidedly less loft than the No. 7 iron (namely 16° as compared to 42°), the sidespin will have more influence on the ball, making the shot more curved horizontally.

In conclusion, we can say that our faults show up more as we progress from the more lofted clubs to the less lofted ones. There is, in fact, so much backspin imparted to the ball with a wedge (No. 10 iron) than an 8° open clubface produces no slice at all, while a 2° open club blade with a driver on a 200-yard drive can put the ball about 20 yards off the target line. So if you want to have a quiet start to a practice session, or if you are loosening up before a round, it is advisable to begin with a wedge or No. 9 iron that is "kind" to you, encouraging a relaxed and free state of mind and movement.

Warming up

But aren't we jumping the gun here? In which other sport involving an athletic movement like a golf swing would one expect the body to jump immediately into action without some form of pre-action warm-up? A sport is a mixture of the technical, physical, and mental—and successful golf is definitely no exception. To be sure of getting off to a good start, whether before a practice session or before playing, a physical warm-up program plays an integral part.

For some reason, probably because of golf's collar-and-tie history, swinging a golf club has not been considered especially energetic or athletic. But countless rounds of golf have been destroyed on the opening holes due to little or no pre-action preparation—not to mention those destroyed towards the end of a round due to physical fatigue. In Chapter 8, Rolf Wirhed goes into more detail concerning the physical aspects of golf, which includes a suggested warm-up program. Read that now, before going further, and help to prevent the risk of physical and mental agonies!

Having now given your body the right basic working conditions, together with the makings of your golf swing and a working knowledge of ball flight, you can now start to practice in a constructive fashion.

46

A page from a practice journal might look like this. Just the act of writing things down can help you to memorize them, but it feels good to have an "extra memory" in a training notebook.

Practice Journal

Date 15 June   Clubs Irons, Nos. 5 and 7   Time

What to train
a) GRIP: get that left-hand-dominating feeling   20 mins

b) Let the arms control the shoulders (relaxed!) on the backswing so that the arms are in a "flatter" position from which to start the downswing.   30 mins

Result
a) Feels more natural. left-hand side of body more in control. Hands fit together better now.

b) Much better when I relax the shoulders at address. Ball starts off more to the right now.

Next session
a) Repeat grip training.
b) Make the address position and "parked" position for the start of the downswing AUTOMATIC. Then train the arm rotation on the downswing to "time" the club blade back to square at impact.

A practice session

If you are still rather uncertain of your striking ability, start by hitting some shots from just off the edge of a practice green. Use a No. 9 iron, with the ball sitting up only a little on a tee or, if the grass is strong enough, sitting "teed up" on the grass. Spend between five and ten minutes with the small pendulum swing, getting a feel of the club, and build up a tempo that feels easy to control. Next, step to the practice hitting area and, with the same club, increase the size of the swing to a half-swing back and through, still with the ball sitting up on a tee or a high-lie. Spend about five minutes and fifteen to twenty shots on this practice, before changing club to a No. 7 iron and moving on to a three-quarter to full-length swing. Stay at that stage for about ten minutes and twenty to twenty-five shots, because you will now begin to notice shot-behavior tendencies in your practice.

At this point, I would like to talk about your general handling of a practice session. In the first place, you must establish a goal for the session, and not get side-tracked. For example, if the purpose of practicing on this particular day is to improve your striking, then don't start to worry about direction or length. Or if you are trying to correct a slice, don't concern yourself with how to increase length. In other words, concentrate your work upon the job at hand and, when you feel that you have made progress, then practice to "program in" the newly-learned thoughts or feelings. Don't move on to something else before the next session.

A notebook is a useful item to have in your golf bag. It can serve as a practice-journal, where you note instructional items received during lessons, or personal thoughts and—most importantly—feelings that bring success during practice. I've heard a story about Joe Carr, top Irish amateur golfer of the fifties and sixties: when he came upon an interesting swing thought, he wrote it down, then cut it out and stuck it onto the top of his driver head. Such a reminder read, "Turn—you idiot!"

Other players have been known to keep several such key thoughts hanging on their golf bags. I think the best place is in your notebook.

The full swing

Now that you have built up to a full swing, I want you to follow some guide-lines as indicated. Establishing the target line makes it easier to identify the two important factors that control the direction of your shots, namely (a) the path of the clubhead at impact and (b) the position of the club blade at impact.

The first factor can be determined by observing the starting-off line of your shots. If the ball starts to the left of the target line, you know that, for some reason, the path of the clubhead when striking the ball was going to the left of the target line. The reverse is also true—a ball starting to the right means a swing path that is moving to the right of the target line.

As for the second factor, we have already seen that the position of the club blade at impact, in relation to the path of the clubhead, will decide whether any sidespin is put on the ball and, if so, which direction the spin and the flight curve will have.

In sum, you will observe two things when hitting your shots: the ball's initial direction, and the eventual curvature that the shot will have as the ball slows down in flight.

By now, you will probably have figured out that there can be only three general starting-off directions for your shots—left, straight, or right—and that there are three possibilities of sidespin for each of these directions: right-to-left, no sidespin at all, or left-to-right. In all, there are nine general shot shapes, no more, and they are shown here.

Of course there are variations on these basic shot shapes. A ball can start more or less to the left or right, and curve to a corresponding degree. But all the shots you hit will generally conform to one of these

nine shapes. A topped shot that doesn't leave the ground will not tell you much about sidespin—but note the ball's rolling direction for swing-path information, tempting though it is to turn away and reach for a new ball!

To lay out guide-lines, decide upon a target, out on the practice area or at the end of it—a length sign, or a tree or house, not too far away. Having done this, lay three or four clubs in a line pointing at the target. This is to be your ball-target reference line. Leave a space where you are going to hit the balls

from: I suggest 2 – 3 yards. Then lay another club behind the space, as an extension of the target line backwards.

When you take golfing lessons, your instructor will probably use the illustrated terms to describe the different-shaped shots. In double-word descriptions, e.g. "push-slice" (shot *i*), the first word describes the initial direction and the second describes the curve that eventually occurs as the ball slows in flight.

Note that the shots curving to the left go longer, because of loft reduction that results from the more closed clubface position at impact.

(*a*) Pull-hook. (*g*) Draw, or hook.
(*b*) Pull. (*h*) Push.
(*c*) Pull-slice. (*i*) Push-slice.
(*d*) Draw.
(*e*) Straight.
(*f*) Fade, or slice.

Topped shots

As we have just mentioned topped shots, let's have a closer look at the "whys and wherefores" of this irritating shot. A so-called "thinned shot" is a topped shot to a lesser degree. Whereas with a full top the ball does not fly due to the lack of backspin, the "thinned shot" may lift because the ball is struck low on the clubface. So the "thinned shot" is a step in between the perfect hit and the full top. There are three types of topped shots, as follows, and we shall assume that both player and ball are on the same ground level.

The perfect strike.

The thinned strike.

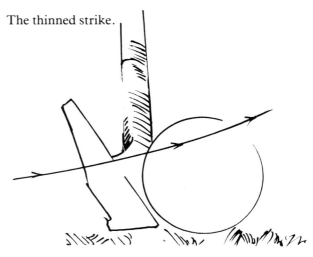

The full top.

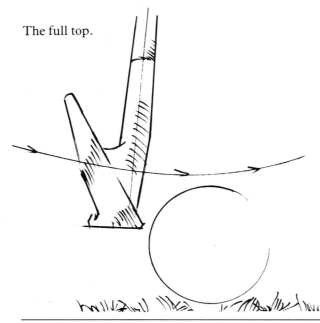

A general word on topped shots: always check the ball position at your preparation before working with your swing. A reason for topped shot 1 can be that the ball is too far to the left from the start. In topped shot 3, a common cause may be having the ball too far to the right at address.

Summary

Swing easy when practicing. A narrow stance more or less forces you to do this, allowing the clubhead's loft to get the ball up into the air. Make sure that you don't look up too early—let it register in your brain that the ball has left the ground, before you check the result. Further, if you practice with shots from a tee, gradually sink the tee as your striking improves, until you can hit directly from the ground.

Topped shot 1

This is very much a beginner's shot, as it arises from the belief that a conscious scooping action is needed to get the ball into the air. On the course, this is often the case where we must fly the ball over something—such as a bunker, tree, or mound.

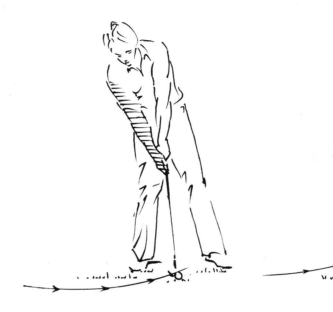

"Swing down, not up" is the key thought for correction here. Don't be afraid to take some turf under, and a little after, the ball. To achieve this, it is important that your left hand/arm dominates on the forward swing until after impact. Activating the right hand breaks the downward path of the clubhead, and increases the risk of striking the top half of the ball.

Drill: Place a tee on the ground directly in front of the ball (target side), and try to "look through" the ball at the tee. Swing down and through, trying to strike the tee. This will result in the clubhead coming low enough under the ball for the blade to create backspin and therefore flight.

Topped shot 2

This is usually a "good" swing path which, for some reason, is simply too high over the ground. A "raising" of the swing center point due to bad balance, often from the swing-preparation position, is one common cause. Another is a straightening of the legs during the downswing, due to *hitting at* the ball instead of *swinging (and turning) through* the ball to a balanced finishing position.

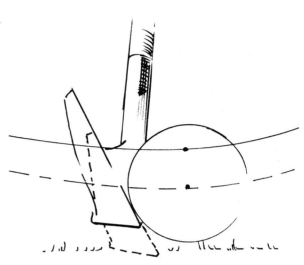

Drill: A build-up of the swing from the first-stage pendulum swing, at an easy pace, thereby putting less stress on the swing center point. Practicing with a very narrow stance, which forces a lower swing tempo in order to keep good balance and control, is an effective drill and generally the one that can help you most to program in correct positions and feelings.

Topped shot 3

This is the better player's topped shot. It is caused mainly by the simple error of a forward (towards the target) movement of the swing center point, creating an early hit on the ball before the clubhead has come low enough in its arc. The major reason for this forward movement is golf's number-one fault, a desire for length. Too much uncontrolled power on the forward swing moves the center point in the same direction as the force, putting the swing out of position in relation to the ball.

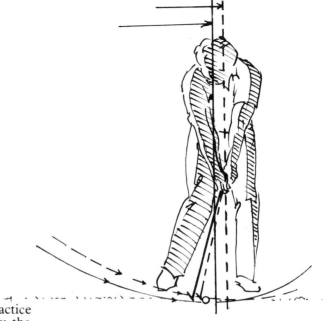

Drills: As with topped shot 2. Moreover, practice from a slightly uphill lie, which will give you the feeling of swinging up through the ball. This is the direct opposite of the situation with this topped

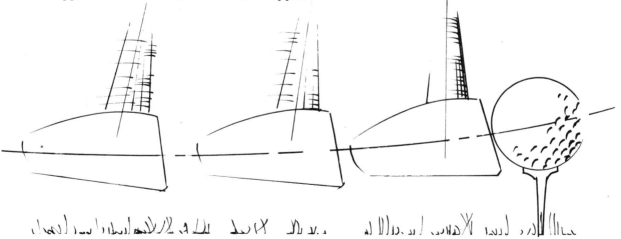

shot, where the ball is being struck on the downward section of the forward swing.

Hitting balls off a high wooden tee with a No. 4 or 5 wood, using a narrow stance, is an interesting drill. Instinctively you begin to swing up more, thus keeping the swing center point in its original place. As all strikes in topped shot 3 are downward swing hits, practice should always be with the ball on a tee. This naturally makes you swing *up* through the ball, whereas a ball lying directly on the ground stimulates a feeling of wanting to hit *down* in order to "dig" the ball out.

Fault analysis and correction

Let's now consider various shot directions and put together a routine for analysis, a list of possible causes, and some drills to facilitate correction. We begin with the two "wrong" directions your shots can have—left and right.

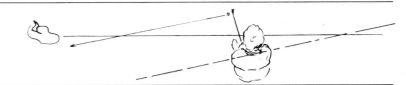

Impact analysis: This tells us that the path of the clubhead is to the left of the ball-to-target line. A ball going to the left of the target line is probably the most common starting line for the average golfer.

Possible reasons

(a) The ball at address is too far to the left, creating an "open" (to the left) shoulder-line position.
To check this: Hold the club in front of you, parallel to the ball-to-target line as described in the line-up check on page 45.
Drill: Go through the line-up procedure on pages 44 – 45.
(b) Allowing the supporting right arm to "overtake" the leading left arm, creating a to-the-left swing path at impact.
To check this: Check the tension in your right hand/arm/shoulder at address. They should be relaxed, to allow the left to dominate on the backswing and to find the top position and the correct plane on the forward swing, so that the clubhead can come in to the ball along the desired path.

Also, check your body posture at address. A too-upright upper body gives too much of a carousel-like shoulder rotation back, and almost always a similar rotation on the forward swing. This results in the clubhead being "thrown" on a path from the outside to the inside of the ball-to-target line (to left) at impact.

Furthermore, check that you start the downswing with the left knee/arm leading. If the left knee (side) is passive, the right swings out and around it, creating a clubhead path towards the left of the target line.
Drills: Lay out parallel clubs forming a track that points to the right of the target line. This visually suggests an inside swing track into the ball. Play some shorter shots, first getting the left arm to lead

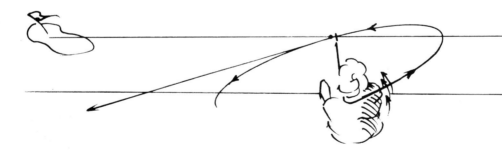

the club in the track on the forward swing, adjusting the angle of the track until the ball starts off along, or slightly to right of, the target line.

Feel the club being "pulled" by the left side and arm along the track, not being "pushed" from the back by the right side. Our golf swing is front-wheel-driven!

Another drill to reduce right-side influence is the so-called "finger-over" grip. As you see, the right hand's control of the club is reduced, due to the thumb and first finger being moved from a holding position to a passive one, thereby increasing the left arm's dominance. This grip, with reduced stability, gives easy shots.

2. STARTING TO THE RIGHT

A ball to the right of the target line is a "good" wrong starting line. This is a positive fault, as the player is coming into the ball in the correct way—but just too much.

Impact analysis: This tells us that the path of the clubhead is to the right of the ball-to-target line.

Possible reasons

(a) The ball at address is too far to the right, giving a "closed" (to the right) shoulder-line position.

To check this: As with the previous line-up fault.

(b) A prolonged left-side dominance on the forward swing, keeping the clubhead along a path from the inside to the outside of the target line for too long.

Drill: Practice programming the body in an open and closing—back and through—fashion. Think of your body as a door that opens on the backswing and closes on the forward swing.

General checkpoint for both of the preceding shots: Check the clubface position at address. If it is open or closed, and at impact the blade has opened or closed even more, this can cause the ball to start to right or left of the target line, even though the path of the clubhead may be correct. In other words, the club-blade position can cancel out the clubhead path's influence on ball flight if it is open or closed enough.

3. STRAIGHT, OR TO LEFT OF THE TARGET LINE, AND THEN "FADING" OR "SLICING" TOWARDS THE RIGHT

Impact analysis: The clubface is open, pointing to the right of the clubhead's swing path at impact.

Possible reasons

(a) Perhaps most commonly, the blade is being held back from rotating by the hands/arms, to compensate instinctively for a swing path that is going towards the left of the target. Because of this swing path, many shots have started to left—and maybe stayed to left—of the target, so that our instinct tries to make the hands steer the blade and the shot more towards the target, giving the blade an open-to-the-path position at impact, and creating a left-to-right (slice/fade) sidespin on the ball. A negative side-effect of this shot is reduced clubhead speed, due to the "holding back" of the clubhead, as well as to the extra loft and the resulting higher flight and reduced length caused by the open blade position.

(b) The position of the hands on the club at your starting position (grip) can affect the clubface position at impact. If the hands (especially the left) are placed too far to the left—the target side of the grip (handle)—then the club blade can be turned open too much during the swing. Thus, when the hands and arms swing back to their natural position at impact, the club blade will be open.

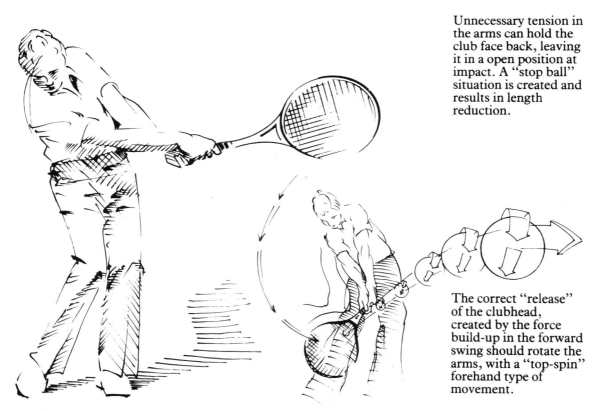

Unnecessary tension in the arms can hold the club face back, leaving it in a open position at impact. A "stop ball" situation is created and results in length reduction.

The correct "release" of the clubhead, created by the force build-up in the forward swing should rotate the arms, with a "top-spin" forehand type of movement.

Drills: If the ball has started its flight to the left of the target line, then your first job is to work on correcting the swing path of the clubhead *(see page 41)*. When this has been corrected, the shot will be a slight push/slice *(see diagram on pages 50 – 51)*. That is, the ball starts a little to the right of the target line, then spins off somewhat to the right of the flight starting line.

Now you can begin to work on correcting the clubface impact position. If, after analysis, you have concluded that the arm/hand rotation mentioned above is at fault, then try the following drill. Separate your hands on the club, with about six inches between them. Slowly practice half-swings a few times, with relaxed arms, noting how rapidly the arms/hands rotate in a scissors movement, the left being forced over by the now more dominant right. This promotes the *feeling* of the correct arm/hand/club blade rotational movement. The movement is the exact opposite of the faulty "stop-ball" blocking position, and can be compared—if we refer to tennis again—to a top-spin forehand. While the "stop-ball" action can be useful in very short shots (pitching), the "forehand" movement is power-releasing when you require length.

Hit some shots from a tee, still with your hands separated. Use a No. 7 or 8 iron, and observe the flight of the ball. It should now fly straighter, or more likely to the left, when you have relaxed properly and allowed the arms to rotate. It feels as if the force produced in the clubhead dominates the movement, thereby rotating the arms/hands and consequently the club blade.

Now hit a few shots with your hands only 2 – 3 inches apart, and relax your arms again until the ball starts to fly straight or curve a little left. Next, use your normal grip, with the same feeling in the arms/hands of rotation created by the clubhead power. This rotation of the arms/hands/club blade should be total, that is, rotating on the drill swing at least 180 degrees from the backswing starting position to the forward swing finishing position. For most golfers who slice, this rotational movement on

the forward swing cannot be too great. It can only start too early (the ball curves to the left) or too late (ball curves to right). The question is now one of timing the rotational movement of the arms/hands so that the club blade arrives at the ball square (pointing at the target) with a straight shot as the result.

If you don't get this result after some practice, check:
(a) that the grip is "within positional limits", with the hands not too far left on the club;
(b) that you are not holding the club too tight, thereby creating too much tension in your arms;
(c) that you are not swinging too fast, and thus, giving the arms/hands too little time in which to allow the clubhead to rotate back to square at impact.

4. STRAIGHT, OR TO RIGHT OF THE TARGET LINE, AND THEN "DRAWING" OR "HOOKING" TOWARDS THE LEFT

Impact analysis: The clubface is closed, pointing to the left of the clubhead's swing path at impact.
Possible reasons
(a) One common reason is that the player is lined-up out to the right from the start, and is therefore forced to rotate the club blade instinctively very early in the forward swing, to prevent the shot from flying in the direction he is lined up in (to the right). This is a deceptive shot, because the player often times it well, and can curve the ball back onto the target—the only problem being that a ball curving so much in this fashion flies lower and rolls more than normally. These effects make control over where the ball finishes somewhat difficult, especially when playing into the green.
(b) Another basic reason for this type of shot, arising often with the better player, is an overdone sideways hip movement on the forward swing. The quest for length frequently makes the better (and younger) player drive forward with the hips, keeping them on a line to the right for too long (blocking). This results in the arms/hands swinging the clubhead along a path from inside the target line to the out-

Driving too hard to the left with the hips will create a blocked position.

Probably golf's most used drill. Here, swinging from a narrow base really tests your swing

balance. If you have been swaying too much, this drill will help program in a more compact,

rotating body movement around your swing center point.

side, creating a shot that starts to the right of the target. As with the previous fault, the player is thus forced to overwork the arms/hands/club blade to curve the ball back towards the target.

In both these cases, the body must "open up"—be turned more towards the target at impact—in order to let the arms swing naturally and freely through the ball, without the need to rotate the club blade earlier than is normal. In the first case, the lining-up procedure described earlier (*pages 44 – 45*) should be adopted, to prevent the swing path from going to the right of the target at impact. After that, the arms can begin to take it easy, and to work on timing the club blade back to the ball as described on page 39.

In the second case, the hips must turn to the left earlier in the forward swing, again to allow freedom for the arms. The following drill can help to program in this movement. Stand with the feet about 6 – 9 inches apart. Now take a full-size swing and try to keep your balance at the end of the movement. Check that the right foot has moved up onto its toe, and that the body has turned with the target-hip square to, and the shoulder a little to the left of, the target. The odds are that, if you have driven forward with the hips too early, you will lose your balance and fall forward (towards the target) when you first try this swing. After some swings your body, which instinctively tries to keep its balance, begins to turn (remember opening and closing the door?) more on the forward swing, giving you a balanced finish and—this being the point of the drill—less sideways hip movement.

(c) A closed clubface at impact can, of course, be caused by your grip, the contact point between the arms and the club blade. This grip, in turn, is influenced by a couple of other basic factors in our start position:

(1) The ball position in relation to the swing center point. If the ball is positioned too far to the left at address, it is natural for the hand to hold the club farther over on the right side (a so-called "strong" grip). This grip, together with a good normal rotation of the arms on the forward swing, *can* cause the club blade to arrive at the ball closed. It is an individual phenomenon. Judy Rankin, one of the best players of modern times on the American LPGA tour, has a very strong grip by normally accepted standards, but still played top golf. However, Judy is an exception—the odds are that you're not.

(2) The same grip effect occurs when the hands at address are pushed too far forward, in front of the ball.

The problem with this grip is that it feels good—that is why it is referred to as strong. Give a club to beginners, and the chances are that, after a few swings, they are holding it in this strong position because they feel that they can generate more power. And indeed they can, because the rotational movement in the arms, discussed above, is brought about more naturally. Alas, often also too extremely, and quickly creating the closed clubface position at impact.

A start position that is too tense (shown here) has a tendency to push the hands under the club (to the right) and can force the ball into a position too much to the left.

Maximizing power

At the beginning of this chapter, I listed the five factors that govern ball flight. The last was concerned with the effect of the club-head's speed upon the shot. The greater this speed is, the more exaggerated are the effects of the other four factors on the ball. For example, a 2° open club blade at impact, with the clubhead travelling at 100 mph, will slice the ball farther off-line than at lower speeds. Logical! Yet what most in-experienced (and even some experienced) players try too often is to hit the long ball without really knowing how power is created, and thereby leaving the swing open to faults in ball contact and shot direction. Let's have a closer look at our golf swing with *controlled creation of power* as our aim.

"Timing" is the order in which the parts move on the forward swing to deliver maximum power to the club head. First the feet; then the thighs, hips, and trunk; finally the arms and club: this is the power-creating sequence of events.

The golfing muscles

At this point, a little explanation about the workings of muscles in our golf swing would be appropriate. I refer you to the following extract from the G.S.G.B. scientific work, "The Search for the Perfect Swing":

A little about the action of the muscles

The common attempt to represent (a golfer swinging) by winding up a big spring in his trunk—however vivid the colours of the drawing—is really very wide of the mark.

In the first place it is untrue simply because a man's muscles are not themselves elastic. When stretched, they just stay stretched, until they are told to contract. Sinews and tendons can provide just a little elasticity at the top of the backswing; and this may indeed make some small contribution to the power of the forward swing. But the main power of the forward swing must come from positive *muscle action.*

Another important property of muscles is that they can only pull, not push. They work by using the bones as levers with which to move the body about. They are thus necessarily arranged in 'antagonistic' pairs, to balance and stabilize each other's action. To make any movement, muscles nearly always work together in groups or sets; and it's a fairly safe bet that in any apparently simple limb movement you care to think of, there will be many more muscles at work than you would ever imagine.

All of them are singly and jointly controlled by co-ordinated electrical impulses sent down nerves from the brain, and they also send back continuous and equally highly co-ordinated information to the brain describing their position and state of tension at any moment. Singly and together they thus function as a highly co-ordinated, versatile and delicately controlled engine to produce force and power.

One other characteristic of the muscles is relevant. The power they give depends on the speed at which they are able to contract. In general, big muscles work at their greatest efficiency, and thus give their greatest power, when working comparatively slowly; whereas small muscles give their peak performance when moving fast.

For all of them, efficient power output depends upon moving the sort of loads at the sort of speeds best suited to them.

Co-ordinating muscles in the right gears

A good example of a man consciously giving his muscles the best sort of loading is a cyclist using his three-speed gear. On the level, where he can bowl along at a reasonable speed, he'll find it costs him least effort to ride in top gear. As he hits a slope, the load increases, his speed falls off, and he finds it less effort to keep up the speed of his leg action by changing to middle gear; and as the hill gets steeper still, down he comes to low gear. Finally, he may find it easier to get off and walk.

Part of the art of the good golfer is that he uses sequences of muscle action so balanced that they enable him to use all the various muscles involved each in the best gear for the job. He will train his central nervous system—his brain and all the nerves in his body together, that is—to co-ordinate all these gearings together in the best possible way to do the job.

All skilled human operations involve and depend on this. The sequence and practicability of the co-ordination in which the muscles work determines power, accuracy and delicacy of control alike.

Which muscles supply the power?

The power required in the golf swing can be calculated, starting from some fairly simple observed facts. We know that the head of a driver weighs about seven ounces; we also know, from film and other measurements, that in a good drive it is accelerated from rest, at the top of the backswing, to just over 100 miles per hour at impact, in a time which can be as short as a fifth of a second. From these figures you can calculate that the average power supplied to the clubhead is about one and a half horse-power.

Of course, when you reach impact the clubhead is not the only thing that is moving; the shaft is, and so are the arms. Indeed the whole body is still turning. This means that power has been supplied to them also. It is not so easy to

Drill 1

(1) Stand firmly with the club stretched out in front of you.

(2) Make a normal backswing, but on a horizontal plane.

(3) Now, with normally relaxed arms and handgrip, swing the arms and club forward and around you again in the horizontal plane. Don't actuate the

hands—just lead the arms and experience the build-up of power in the clubhead, *without* having to use your hands consciously to help. The dominating force here is

centrifugal, and you release it when you lead with the arms, allowing the force to explode with conscious effort from your hands.

calculate this power, because we don't know exactly how heavy any given part of the body is, or how fast it is moving at impact; but it is fairly safe to say that at least an equal amount of power, a further one and a half horse-power, is used in this way, giving a total of three horse-power, and probably more, for the whole downswing.

This power must come from muscles; and we can calculate how much muscle is involved. Working at their best possible loading (in the 'right gear' as we put it earlier) muscles are known to produce a maximum of about an eighth of a horsepower per pound of muscle. In the average man the total weight of all the muscles acting in and on the arms is about twenty pounds, of which only about half can produce useful power at a given instant, on account of their arrangement in opposing pairs.

Roughly speaking, therefore, the power available from the arms amounts at most to one and a quarter horse-power, and is probably less, since loading cannot be optimal throughout the whole duration of the downswing. Clearly, if we are looking for three to four horse-power, we must go to our biggest muscles, those of the legs and lower body, for the main supply of power. In fact, the muscles acting in and on the legs weigh about forty pounds and can produce two and a half horse-power or so.

Thus, without even considering the detailed

movements in a golf swing, we can make a fundamental and far-reaching statement about it: that the muscles of the legs and hips constitute the main source of power in long driving.

This is not to deny the importance of hands, arms, shoulders, or any other specific part; but they *are* important primarily because any sequence of linked movements is only as good as its weakest point. Make no mistake: **the legs and hips are the 'engine' of the swing; the arms and hands are the transmission system**—albeit one in which a certain amount of extra power can be added. Strong hands may be needed *for big hitting, but they are not the primary power source.*

The main mistake made by many short-hitting players is to activate the clubhead with the hands in a kind of "throwing" movement, as one of the first movements of the forward swing. The illustrated drills (above and on the following page) should help you to develop the right kind of feeling when you start the forward swing.

The lateral hip movement on the forward swing is something that many golfers, especially youngsters, tend to overdo. Maybe it is those swing-sequence pictures which one sees often in golf magazines and books, that are to blame—or else it is just the natural urge to "get at the ball and give it

Drill 2
(1) Turn the club upside-down, holding the shaft just above the clubhead.
(2) Now take a normal swing, noting that there is a swishing sound from the fast-moving grip-end of the club. Swing two or three times again, and note the part of your swing arc where the sound is loudest. If you are "out of sequence" in your forward movement, the loudest point will be somewhere else than just in front of you—where the ball usually lies. For anxious early hitters, the sound will be before the hitting area; for late or non-hitters, it will be after you've passed the ball, and probably with a quieter swish.

a whack". Whatever the reason behind this movement, two major problems arise:
(1) The swing center point can be forced to move forward (towards the target), creating too much of a downward hit on the ball. This results in a topped or thinly-hit shot when the ball is lying directly on the ground, or frequently a "skied" shot when the ball is teed up.
(2) The hips get "locked" in the sideways position, blocking the way through the ball for the following arms and shoulders. This produces either a pushed shot or a pulled shot.

The hip movement on the forward swing, therefore, is an initial sideways thrust that develops into a rotation—a sideways kick with the hips that can still allow the body to turn around the center axis of the swing.

Chapter 3
PUTTING

A twenty-handicap golfer, when playing to his or her handicap on a course with par seventy-two, takes ninety-two strokes. Of this total the player has—and I am probably being generous here—thirty-six putts, averaging two putts per green. In other words, almost 40% of all the shots played are putts. A top professional golfer, while playing a trouble-free seventy-stroke round, has approximately thirty-two putts, or 45%. Indeed, no other club is certain to be used as often as the putter.

The professional player knows this, and devotes a high proportion of his practice time to putting. A twenty-handicapper knows it too, but very often brushes off such thoughts with statements such as "You can't learn putting—it's individual", "You're either born with it or you're not", "It's so boring to practice putting", "Our practice putting green is not at all like the greens on the course", and so forth. Yet the observation "I played the longer shots well, but on and around the greens I was terrible" is probably the most often-heard complaint at the 19th hole.

During my twenty-three years of teaching golf, perhaps at most a hundred pupils have come and asked for a putting lesson. The reason, I believe, is that many players feel the degree of difficulty in striking the ball with a putter to be low compared with, say, using a wooden club—and of course they are right. So time and money are spent on the longer game in the initial stages of learning, and then the short game—as play on and around the greens is referred to—gets relegated to the "I can teach myself" approach. This can cost further time and anguish, in some cases even frustration leading to quitting the game altogether. Hitting a drive out of bounds may be accepted with a laugh, but taking three or four putts on a fast green feels very humiliating.

In my view, the most complete and efficient way to learn to play golf is the way described in Chapter 1, building up from the smaller, simpler, confidence-developing movements. Thus, the "short game" is *not* a separate game, but an area where more variations on the main swing theme can be built in.

If you have followed the swing-building program outlined earlier in the book, then you have a basic putting movement. The simple arms/hands/club pendulum swing with no wrist-break gave us
  —confidence in striking the ball
  —a movement dominated by the left arm
  —a swing *through* the ball *at* the target
  —a balanced tempo
  —a general swinging, rather than hitting movement.
In sum, all ingredients that comprise a reliable putting stroke. Why, you may ask, should we do anything more as regards the actual movement?

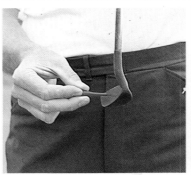

To find your putter's best striking point, hold it between your thumb and forefinger, so that it hangs balanced. Take a wooden tee and, starting at the toe end, tap the putter blade along its center line, ½ inch at a time, moving towards the club heel. You will notice that the blade turns and vibrates out on the toe. This effect decreases as you approach the

Well, when we started to build the swing, we were going step by step towards a full swinging movement. Our initial pendulum swing was created with a larger finished product in mind: a free movement to get the parts involved moving in the right order, along the right lines, through the right positions. The on-course putting stroke differs somewhat. It is limited in movement and in size, and should be constructed—as far as possible—to withstand any eventual negative mental effects. Therefore, a "tightening up" of our basic pendulum movement, and the establishment of an orderly process for successful putting, should now be made.

Principles of putting

Let's refer back to the five laws of ball flight, which apply to a great extent here, even though in putting the ball is on the ground for the most part. They concern:

1. The clubface contact point with the ball at impact.
2. The clubhead's angle of approach at impact.
3. The clubhead's path at impact.
4. The clubface angle to the swing path at impact.
5. The clubhead's speed at impact.

As we have found earlier, if all of these factors are judged to be correct, then a successful shot has been produced. Other than these, it is only the hard-to-gauge external factors, such as weather and grass, that can affect the result. We shall now take the laws in turn and discover the principles of putting.

1. The ball must be struck on the "sweet-spot" of the putter blade in order to maintain a constant strength of hitting.

Exactly as with the longer shots, we must strive towards perfect strikes and, in putting, this means knowing where the "perfect" striking point is on the putter blade. The point can, however, vary between putter models. Many have a line or setter etched onto the blade's top or front. This, on well-known brands, can be relied upon to show the designed hitting point. But on cheaper models, a line is often only a cosmetic marking and cannot be depended on for accuracy. Make a test with your own putter as illustrated here.

Strikes at a point off the sweetspot (less than 100% solid contact) will leave the ball somewhat short of the target and off-line (as the blade can turn, depending on the strength of hit and the stability of your grip).

2. The club blade should strike the ball at the bottom of the swing arc with a normal lofted putter.

"sweetspot", then increases after it. So the "sweetspot" is the point where the blade feels the most solid. Compare that point with the marking on the club, if any, or make a new mark above that point with some tape, a pen, or a metal saw.

Striking the ball on the up or downswing will mean contact low or high on the club blade, thereby missing the sweetspot. It will also mean a chance of loft at impact. The upswing hit can make the ball fly into the air a little at first, and this, together with the off-center strike, leaves the ball short. The downswing hit gives a reduced loft, and can push the ball downwards into the green, causing an undesired influence on the putt from the ground—namely resistance and loss of power—and even some backspin effect which, again, results in a shorter putt than was planned.

Striking the ball with the blade travelling parallel to the green at impact will propel the ball forward, initially with some skidding movement (no spin), then with line-holding topspin, and of course with increased chances of striking the sweetspot.

3. The clubhead at impact must be travelling along the desired starting line of the putt.

Due to the club's short length and upright lie (the angle between shaft and clubhead sole), the natural swing path for the clubhead is close to being along the shot's starting line. We have to make sure that, with our set-up position, alignment, and movement, we utilize this advantage.

4. The club blade's position at impact must be at 90° to the swing path of the clubhead.

Topspin, a vertical rotation of the ball, is vital if:

(a) The ball is to have the best possible chance of staying on its starting line.

(b) A ball that strikes either edge of the hole is to have the best possible chance of dropping in.

(c) External factors such as the grain of the green are to have minimum influence on the direction of the putt as intended.

(d) The ball is to be hit solidly as intended (an open or closed club blade would create a somewhat glancing strike and give reduced length).

5. The clubhead's speed at impact must be within certain limits that are required by the length of the putt.

This law probably has the greatest control over how many putts the average golfer takes for each green. An average-size golf green is about 100 feet long and 75 feet wide. When we consider that putting is sometimes necessary from beyond the edge of the green, it becomes all the more clear that strength of putting is vitally important to low scoring. Our putting swing must have, within its range of movement and tempo, the capability of hitting the ball up to perhaps the full length of the green.

So there we have the criteria for construction of a putting swing. Add to these the external factors—deciding the slope of the green, the effects of grass and wind, the mental pressures of competition, and the brainwork of collecting everything together in a calculated movement—and we face an interesting challenge. It is certainly one that will be as exciting to master as are the game's longer shots, and therefore it should be worth spending some time on.

Preparing and swinging

Let us start with the grip, stance, and posture which we had when we began to build our golf swing. The grip had the left hand on the left side of the shaft, and the right hand directly opposite, with the palms square to each other and to the club blade. The thumbs were on top of the shaft, lying on the flat part of the grip, and the right hand was holding directly under the left hand in the so-called baseball two-fisted grip. Our criteria for putting require a stable, controlled movement. Thus, our contact point with the club must be an important factor in achieving this stability. The hands and arms in the putting stroke, ideally, need to be locked into a system that is free from nervousness and uncertainty.

We have established that we want the club blade at impact to be square and travelling on the line which the ball should start rolling along. If we were to choose a model to represent this, it would be the ferris wheel we spoke of in Chapter 2—it moves constantly along the same path and has one end square to the path. Now our normal golf swing leaves this path on the backswing, comes back onto it on the forward swing, and then leaves it again. The arms rotate back and through, in order to swing further and to create a high clubhead speed. But we need neither of these features in putting. So let's see if we can avoid them and thereby stabilize our putting stroke, by adjusting the way in which we hold the putter (as in the illustration).

The effects of this new way of holding the putter are twofold:

(*Above and opposite, upper left*) Start with the grip, stance, and posture described on page 14.

—The hands are now under the shaft in a position to counteract the unwanted opening and closing of the club blade in the putting stroke, satisfying law 4.

—For the same reason, the clubhead is less likely to leave the intended starting line for the putt, satisfying law 3.

The arms are now closer to the body than previously, and this helps to create a stable, compact movement. It may feel somewhat stiff and mechanical at first, but don't forget that "mechanical" is what we are striving for in our putting stroke—a foolproof method.

A word about grip pressure. The general rule for many years has been that one should hold a putter lightly. Comparisons with egg-holding, birds, and other delicate objects have been used, probably because skilful

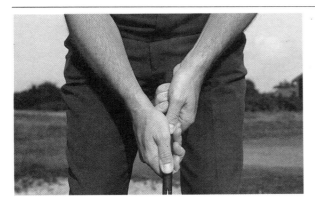

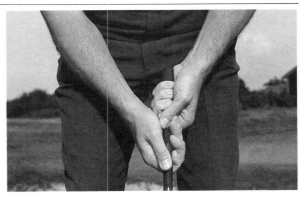

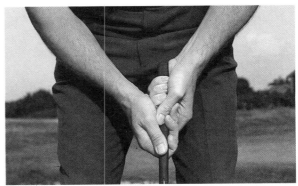

(*Upper right*) Allow both hands to slide under the shaft.

(*Lower left*) Raise the index finger of your left hand, allowing the little finger of the right hand to fit snugly under.

(*Lower right*) The hands are now under the shaft, positioned opposite each other, keeping each other in check, with the blade locked square.

top golfers do this. In my experience, it is not always the best rule—in fact, I believe that many weekend players would create a more reliable putting stroke with the strength of their normal grip. The latter would prevent uncontrolled movement in the wrists, and therefore out in the clubhead, as well as holding up better under pressure in competition. I feel also that there should be more pressure in the left hand, the leading side in our swing, while the right hand continues its support-to-left-arm role as in the larger swing.

A side-effect of our grip change is that it will be natural to bend more from the hips, allowing the arms to go out more at the elbows, which gives greater freedom of movement.

The width between the feet can now be increased, creating a more steady base, and locking the legs at the knees towards each other as if a plastic bucket were trapped between them. This locking of the body, from the waist downwards, assists in our goal of a simple arm/putter movement from the shoulders. Thus, as with the longer shots, tension in the upper half of the body is to be avoided.

The adjustment of bending forward more from the waist helps us to bring our head, and consequently our eyes, into a position more directly over the ball-to-target line. This gives us a bird's-eye view along the path that the clubhead should follow back and through the ball. An eye position too far outside this line will tend to promote an outside-to-inside swing path, pulling the putt towards the left, while an eye position

Try the plastic-bucket trick to check how the locked lower half of your body should feel.

Test your own eyes-over-target line position, by addressing the ball and then holding another club so that it forms a vertical line hanging from the eyes: check whether it is pointing at, outside, or inside the target line. Another way of testing is to drop a ball from the eye position after you take the stance, and note where it hits the ground in relation to the target line.

too far inside can produce an opposite error.

While on the subject of contact with the target, it is worth noting that many good putters stand slightly open, with the body and feet-line diverging to the left of the target line, in order to get a better target contact. After all, the best contact that we have with an object or person is from a facing position. Precision target games such as darts or bowling are played from this position. I would like to recommend that the longer putts are played with an open starting position, whereas the shorter putts are played with a "square" stance that keeps the line across the toes parallel to the target line.

We are now set to swing. Check that the arms and club feel as if they are one, that the wrists are stable and the arms free at the shoulder joints. Swing the putter back slowly, and accelerate through the ball—*at least* as far through as you swung the club back. It is safer to have a shorter backswing and make a positive movement on the forward swing, than to have a long backswing and feel forced to decelerate as you swing towards the ball.

Probably the most important element in putting—indeed in all golf—is tempo. We lose accuracy if we lose tempo. Finding the tempo that suits you is a matter of trial-and-error as well as instinct. Specifically, tempo

Ball position is an important thing to check. Ball-flight law 2 stated that we must strike the ball at the bottom of the swing arc. of it. If we were to swing one-armed, our bottom point would be where the clubhead is now, directly under the left shoulder. But when we add the stabilizing right hand and arm, we pull back the arc's bottom to a point . . . well, find it yourself. Swing a few opposite the center of the left shoulder. It suits us fine, because we can naturally allow the head to be turned slightly to the left to see the ball,

How do we know where that is? Take the putter in the left hand, and allow the arm to hang straight down, feeling the club as an extension times, and feel where the blade brushes the grass. This is where you should position the ball.

This point will probably be about and can "feel" better where the target is than if the head were turned away from the target.

means accelerating the clubhead at the right rate, to reach the speed required by law 5. The slower your tempo is, the farther you must swing the club in order to reach that speed—and the faster your tempo is, the less easily you can control the clubhead. The correct tempo for you is one that is not so slow that you are always forced to take long swings to get the ball up to the hole, and not so fast that your control over the clubhead is too finely balanced. Your tempo should remain constant for all but the really long putts, leaving the length of backswing to control the length of putt. Only at the maximum backswing length, where you feel that it is uncomfortable and unnatural to

swing farther with your locked-wrist pendulum movement, should you speed up the tempo of your swing in order to hit the ball further.

At a greater distance from the hole, when you are outside the green or putting far uphill, you may feel that it is more natural to let your wrists break a little on the backswing, so as to gain clubhead speed. This is rather individual, and I recommend some experimentation—a faster tempo with stiff wrists, or the usual tempo with a wrist break on the backswing (or perhaps a mixture of the two!).

On long putts, stand slightly open (with your toes pointing slightly forward), and you will feel that you have better contact with the target.

READING THE GREENS

The observant golfer starts to "read" the green when he or she is walking towards it. Follow the steps described in the illustrations and you will acquire enough information to be in a position to make a good putt when your turn comes up.

1 The general slope of the green is often easier to see when you are 50 yards away, than when you are standing in the middle of it.

2 Next, walk around the side of the green to get a view of the putt line from behind the flag.

3 Now go behind the ball and view the line.
   Thus, by the time you reach the ball, you have checked the putt from two angles.

4 Now, look at the putt to be played from the side.

5 If your playing partners are to putt first, watch how their putts have rolled; see how hard they struck the ball, and whether it rolled more or less than you thought it would. In this way, you can get an idea of the "strength" of the slope and of the grass from that direction.

When it is your turn to play, go out to the side of the putt, and "feel" the length. Without delaying play, take a practice swing that you feel to be the correct size and tempo, while looking at the putt line.

1

One of the pleasures of golf is that no two courses are the same. Greens differ in both contour and quality, and even in type of grass. After you have tried your home course, you come to imagine a certain standard for greens, and on this you base your judgement for "the greens of the day" while playing on your home course, as well as when visiting other courses. The time of year is a major influence, but the recent weather conditions and the cut of the grass are further factors that must be taken into consideration when planning a putt. In warmer climates, there is often a strong nap with the types of grass found on greens. An identification of such grass can be made by changes of shade, like those seen on well-kept lawns. When the grass is running away from you, the shade is lighter and you can expect the ball to roll farther—even, in some cases, against the apparent slope of the green. The darker shades indicate that the grain is growing towards you, with a braking effect on the putt.

It is advisable to check the last few feet of a longer putt, where the ball is going to slow down and, therefore, become more susceptible to the direction of the grain. In fact, examining the edges of the hole, and noting whether there is any pronounced grain direction, can be of assistance. On summer greens, where artificial watering is necessary, the color of the grass indicates green speed. The lighter shades of green will be faster than the darker, more lush areas.

A former NASA scientist and now golf technical consultant, Dave Pelz, has researched putting very thoroughly, and has arrived at the conclusion that the ideal strength for a putt is one which, if it didn't go in, would roll 17 inches past. The reasons are:

(a) A return putt of this length is not too difficult.
(b) With this strength, the ball is less influenced by the grain and the slope.
(c) With this strength, a slightly off-hole center putt can be turned into the sides of the cup.

All putts are straight!
To most successful professional players, all putts are played as if they were straight. After summarizing the slope and speed of the putt, a picture is formed in the mind's eye of the successful result. Visualize the whole putt from the start until the ball drops into the hole. To do this, some reference points along the way would help. These may be blemishes in the grass, differences of shade, repaired pitch marks, or anything else that can help to picture the finished putt.

In all four situations shown here, a point has been taken along a continuation of the ball starting-line, as if, in our imagination, the hole had been moved to that point. The putt is played as if it were going straight to the "imagined hole," allowing the slope or the grain to turn the ball off this line towards the actual hole.

Situation 1:

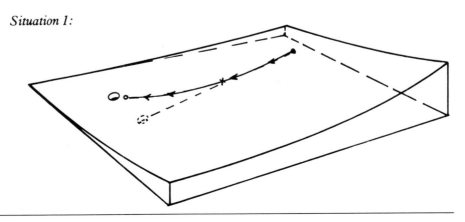

Situation 2:

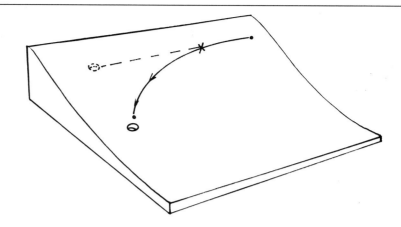

Situation 3:

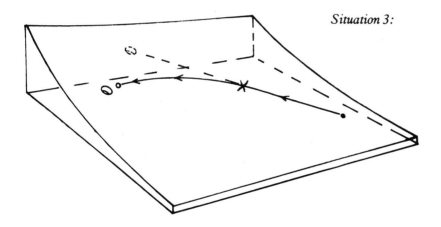

Situation 4:

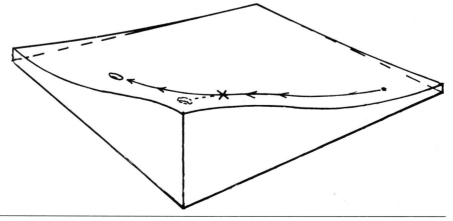

Practicing putting

Drill 1: *"Railway Track"*
Lay two clubs parallel to each other and up to the hole, leaving just enough space between them for the width of the putter head plus ½ inch at each end. The ball is positioned about halfway along the clubs from the hole, and midway between them. With the clubs acting as a guide track, you can check:

(*a*) that you are keeping the clubhead along the track to the target through the ball-striking area, (4 inches on either side of the ball) parallel to the clubs;

(*b*) that the club

blade is kept at right angles to the track.

After you have holed 10 putts in a row, move the clubs one club-length from the hole, and repeat the drill. This time, you must sink 8 out of 10 putts.

Next, move the clubs at one-club-length intervals farther from the hole, and reduce the score of holed putts by one each time. The other putts must be past the hole, and by no more than 17 inches.

The first series should be straight putts, on a flat part of the practice green. Then your own fantasy can create a goal-setting program on the sloping parts of the green.

Drill 2: *"Hurdles"*
Lay out 6 – 7 clubs at about 1-yard intervals. Stand approximately 5 yards away from the first club, and decide which distance you are going to putt. For example, if you decide on the fifth club, then the ball must stop within a half a yard of that club in order to be "approved." Vary the order in which you take the distances—just as you do when you putt in actual play.

The point of this drill is to associate the correct backswing length with the distance to the target, preferably with a constant swing tempo. Practice first on a flat part of the green, then uphill and finally downhill putts.

Drill 3: *Steep downhill putts*
If you have to play on fast undulating greens where you get steep downhill putts, and if you feel afraid even to touch the ball because it will roll past, try this drill. Instead of hitting the ball off the clubhead's sweetspot, hit it towards the toe. This produces a less solid hit on the blade, without

your having to reduce the backswing with un-rhythmical movement.

Don't be afraid that the blade will turn to the right and roll the ball off line. Just hold the club a little more firmly, and the blade will stay square. This allows us to keep a positive swing movement despite the "slippery" green. The red line shows the sweetspot.

Drill 4: *Short-putt "zoom-in"*
Concentration is important for all shots, but especially for putting. Putts of a yard or less can make the wildest thoughts go through the head of even the most experienced tournament pro. Check that the line

of your putt is normal, and decide which point of the hole's circumference the ball is to roll over. Then "zoom in" with your eyes on that point, and concentrate on rolling the ball right over that point. See how close you can get to it, and I'll bet that by

"zooming in" you will seldom miss so badly that the ball fails to go in the hole.

Drill 5: *"Parking the long shot"*
On putts of about 10 yards and more, we are normally satisfied with a safe two-putt finish. Looking at a little hole from longer distances can create unnecessary tension and hamper our free putting stroke.

Place three clubs around the hole at about 30 inches from it—one behind the hole and one at each side, forming a

"parking place" around the hole. Suddenly the target area will look quite easy to reach, making you relax and allowing a freer movement. After you have practiced putting balls into this parking place for a while, you can imagine the same place in a relaxed way when you get a long putt out on the course.

Summary of a successful putting routine

1. Observe the general contours as you approach the green.
2. Check the putt line from behind the hole as you go past the green.
3. Stop and check the putt length and slope from the side as you go to the ball.
4. Check the line from behind the ball.
5. Visualize a successful putt with the help of intermediate targets (check points).
6. Pick out a point where you judge that the ball will start to swing. Imagine a line from the ball out through that point, extending to a "moved hole" as far away as the real hole.
7. Without aiming, take a couple of practice swings that you feel are the right size and tempo for the putt length.
8. Aim the club blade at the "imagined hole" and take up your putting stance.
9. Focus your eyes on the ball, then turn your head so that your eyes follow the planned putt route through the intermediate targets into the "imagined hole."
10. Play the putt without delay.

Chapter 4
UP AND DOWN AROUND THE GREEN

So far, the high-handicap (= weekend) golfer has, by following our program, equipped him- or herself with two swing movements:

(*a*) The single-lever swing, in which the arms and the club form a one-piece unit. This we used as the first stage in our swing-building process, and again—in a modified version—in the previous chapter about putting.

(*b*) The two-lever swing, in which the left arm and the clubshaft act upon each other through the hinge at the wrists. We use this swing for all shots requiring more power than the simpler, more controllable single-lever pendulum swing can produce.

If it were at all possible to hit a 250-yard drive with the single-lever swing, then we would have a greater control over our shots, and would have no use for the risky two-lever swing—until we want to hit a 400-yard drive! Thus, when we begin to look at some of the shorter shots around the green, our first thought should be: "Can we use the more reliable single-lever swing in this situation?"

When playing short shots, a controlled movement is paramount for accuracy. The single-lever swing is a step in that direction. Another is the choice of club. Suppose you have a shot from 5 yards outside the green, and the flag is at the back of the green, giving a total shot length of 25 – 30 yards, while there is no bunker or rise in the way and the green slopes lightly from back to front (towards you). It is very tempting to pick a wedge out of the bag and fly the ball into the air with a wristy (two-lever) swing, thereby pitching the ball a few yards short of the hole, and hope that it stops just right to finish near the hole. Now let me say one thing straightaway: if you can get the ball within 1.5 yards of the hole at least 80% of the time, then just keep on playing that shot—and think about becoming a pro as well! But the weekend golfer will not normally be able to make this fine a wedge shot, so he has to think again, and the following will help him.

What I want to do here is present some principles that can help in deciding which type of shot involves the least amount of risk-taking. Which club in the bag is the simplest to control? The answer, of course, is the putter. Why?

(*a*) It is the shortest club, and therefore easiest in gaining control over the clubhead.

(*b*) There is no loft to speak of, so we avoid having to judge how much the shot will brake during the first couple of bounces.

(*c*) Because of its lack of loft, the putter can hit the ball a reasonable distance without having to take too long a backswing.

(*d*) We use the single-lever swing.

All this makes golf sound as if we don't need more than one club to play with. But the putting principle serves us well until we must get the ball over something, or for some reason want it to stop quickly. The same goes for the single-lever swing—it is fine until we need to gain speed in the clubhead to create length or backspin.

Based on the above observations, our short-shot philosophy should be this:

in all situations we try to use the least lofted club for the job, together with the shortest backswing.

I'm sure you will understand more as we look in detail at the different situations I have lined up for you. But first a little about pre-shot procedures.

As soon as we move outside the green, the first noticeable difference is that the lie of the ball can vary. The surface may, with a little luck, be just as good as the green. But the ball may instead lie down in grass, or in a place with virtually no grass at all. It may even lie on sand or on a slope, in a spot where someone else has played a shot, or on a pathway.

So, to begin with, the position of the ball on the ground decides to a certain extent what we are able to do with the ball. Secondly, we must look at the target area where we want the ball to finish. With these starting and finishing positions, the next step is to see how the area between them looks. This pattern of observation is the basis for visualizing the desired shot in your situation. Let's go through the process to understand its principles.

The lie of the ball

For purposes of instruction, I will divide the way the ball lies into three categories: good, half-good, and bad.

A good lie exists when any club in the set, regardless of loft, can strike the back of the ball and make it fly or roll without hindrance. A good lie can be found anywhere on the course. If you see a good player going into the rough with a wooden club, it is because he has been fortunate enough to get a good lie.

A half-good lie (note the positive tone!) exists when the ball is lying somewhat down in the grass, and can only be struck cleanly on the back with a limited range of clubs—probably from a No. 5 or 6 iron down.

A bad lie is a situation where, if we are at all able to strike the back of the ball, it is only by using the most lofted clubs in the set: No. 9 iron, pitching wedge, and sand wedge. In extremely bad lies, the possibility of gaining relief through the "unplayable ball" rule should be considered.

The deeper the ball lies in the grass, the steeper the swing's angle of attack into the ball must be. This is automatically aided by the choice of club. The shorter the club's length, the steeper the approach angle that the clubhead naturally has into the ball. Not only that—the shorter the club is, the greater the loft.

All this may sound as if we have skipped a chapter and are already discussing trouble shots. But the first step in planning a successful golf shot is an analysis of the lie of the ball, and that can vary even on the fairway. The good lie usually presents no problems to playing a normal golf shot, as there is direct (clean) contact between the club and ball. When the ball lies deeper, there may be some grass trapped between the ball and club blade at impact. The amount of grass may be seen when you place the clubhead behind the ball (but be careful not to move the ball or you will get a penalty stroke!). How much resistance the grass will give is a question of judgement based on practice and experience. Obviously, the thicker the grass, the greater the resistance.

An important effect on the shot played from such half-good or bad lies is that the clubface puts less spin on the ball. The grass forms, so to speak, a protective cover. This is why it is sometimes difficult to control the length of longer shots ("fliers") played from such lies, while shorter shots played with the lofted clubs lack some of their normal

Good lie   Half-good lie   Bad lie

backspin and have little stopping force when they hit the green. This "flier" effect is accentuated when the grass is "juicy" due, for example, to rain or watering.

Another aspect of lie is that it is easier to put backspin on the ball, and thus to stop it

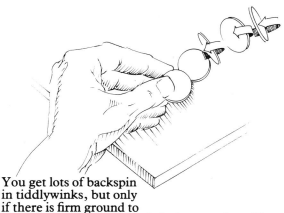

You get lots of backspin in tiddlywinks, but only if there is firm ground to push against.   It is the same in golf!

from rolling too much, when the ball is lying on firm ground. Think of the children's game, tiddlywinks. Pressing down on the counter to make it jump into the air requires something hard beneath it to press against, creating maximum backspin and resultant lift. Therefore, a shot played from a lie up in the grass, or on soft ground, will have less stopping force.

You can see, then, that the ball's lie has a great influence upon the choice of shots available.

The target area

We now shift our attention to the green and check the factors that will affect our shot-planning. Having analyzed the lie of the ball, we know more about options that are open to us from that standpoint. What sort of information are we seeking when we examine the target area?

(1) Is the green hard or soft? As with putting, observe other players' shots if they play first. Check how the ball reacted if it was pitched onto the green. Did it "bite"

(brake on the first or second bounce), and how much did it roll? If you can do so without delaying the play, go forward and check the texture of the green when you walk on it, especially the area where you feel that you will want to pitch the ball.

(2) How does the green slope? If it runs downhill away from you, there may be more roll on your shot. Uphill, the opposite is true—more stopping effect. Sideways slopes should be treated as when putting.

(3) Is the hole situated so that it would be preferable to have an easier uphill putt left after your approach shot? If so, then re-plan your target area.

(4) Is the hole located close to a problem area (such as a bunker, rough, or steeply arched edge of the green)? The longer the shot to be played, the greater is the margin for error to be considered. For most golfers, a long putt is easier than a short bunker shot.

(5) Are you playing up or down to the green? If the green is higher up than the player, then the ball obviously must fly high—but it comes down to earth relatively soon, thus reducing the shot's length. Playing to a green that is lower will often demand a high shot, but the ball will fly longer, staying in the air for a greater time before hitting the ground.

This analysis of the target area presents a picture of the shot that is required. The analysis of the ball's lie tells us what sort of shot is possible. If we now add information about the area in between, things become clearer. Is this area level or undulating? Is there a bunker or water to be played over? We can thereby begin to imagine the ball trajectory needed, and the type of shot and choice of club to be used.

Let's now look at some situations and, armed with our set of clubs and two golf swings, see if we can define the necessary shots. We will start with a series of positions that lie close to the green's edge, no farther than 25 – 30 yards from the hole.

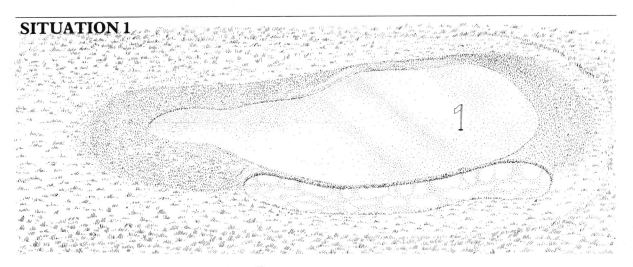

Analysis

The ball lies well on the apron. The flag stands in a small area on a plateau. The green slopes off to the right, down towards a bunker. In between, the green is well-kept and has a clear slope uphill to the plateau.

Shot picture

As the ball lies well, and the grass between the ball and the edge of the green is quite short, we can use the club that we have the greatest control over—the putter. We should roll the ball to the left of the hole, because the plateau's bank will swing the ball to right, and the green also slopes to right. Since there is an opposing slope onto the plateau, it is important not to go too far past the hole, which would leave us with a downhill putt back towards the bank. So we want to putt about 40 inches to the left of the hole and, if anything, somewhat short of it.

Technique/club choice

A long putt with maximum swing length—and perhaps with increased tempo, depending on how fast your standard tempo is. Single-lever swing. A harder than normal shot is required, due to the braking effect of the plateau bank and to the uphill slope of the plateau itself.

This is a variation of the first situation, the difference being that the ground between the ball and the edge of the green is uneven, making putting risky. A rolling ball could strike one of the ridges and take away too much of the shot's power or change its direction. Such a position requires that the ball be lifted over the uneven area, so that its first bounce is 2 – 3 feet into the green. From there, the ball should run as if it had been putted.

In sum, the ball ought to be in the air for about 4 yards, and on the ground for about 25 yards with the last few yards slightly uphill. This shot picture indicates the use of a low lofted iron, type No. 4 or 5, if we are to keep our swing as short as possible and let the club do the work for us. So let's look at the technique for such a shot.

The first thing we notice is, of course, that the 4/5 iron is longer than a putter, if we hold it normally. Therefore, to begin with, we try to handle the iron club as a putter. After all, the only quality the iron has that interests us is its loft. We hold it further down so the distance between the grip and the clubhead is as with a putter. Stand up to the ball, imitating your putting style as closely as is comfortable, the main difference being your body position relative to the ball.

When chipping—as this shot is called—the address position should be taken with the ball more to the right than when putting. This will help to put your hands slightly in front of the ball, encouraging a steeper swing angle into the ball, and promoting direct club/ball contact. This ball-position adjustment is also necessary in situations where the ball is lying down in the grass, so that the swing angle of attack must be steeper in order for the club to get at the back of the ball and continue underneath to lift it.

Analysis

The ball lies well, relatively near (about 3 yards from) the edge of the green. The hole is downhill from the ball, only 5 yards in on the green. To the left of the hole, the green slopes off down into sand.

Shot picture

Aim slightly to right, because of the slope. The ball should go up in the air, and bounce on the green with "brakes on" so that it doesn't run too far past the hole, although an uphill second putt is preferred. The total shot length is short, requiring a low club-head speed, but also a backspin effect.

Technique/club choice

Single-lever swing with lofted club, to create height and, more importantly, backspin—probably around a No. 9 iron/wedge.

Analysis

The ball lies well on the fairway (about 10 yards from the edge of the green) but the grass is a little long. There is some uneven ground, 4 – 5 yards from the green edge. The hole is 10 yards in on the green, which slopes down from the left and, behind the hole, slopes away down into a bunker.

Shot picture

The ball rises over the fairway grass and apron. Its first bounce is 1 yard into the green, on a line to left of the hole. It brakes a bit to slow down the shot, leaving enough roll for the ball to reach the hole, preferably a little short and to the right (for an uphill second putt).

Technique/club choice

Medium lofted iron, No. 7 or 8, to obtain a little backspin. This provides the power needed to get the ball over the uneven ground into the green, while the loft is sufficient to give the required braking effect. Again, the single-lever putting action is adequate and more reliable.

Analysis

The lie of the ball is half-good, lying down a little in the grass and about 6 yards from the edge of the green. The flag is quite close to the edge of the green, which slopes downhill.

Shot picture

Because of the ball's nearness to the green and the downhill slope, we need a quickly rising high shot that will have a lot of backspin, so that the slope will not roll the ball too far.

Technique/club choice

The ball's position down in the fairway grass can reduce the backspin effect. We must therefore, with our choice of club and swing technique, try to create as much backspin as possible, to get the ball as high as we can and, thus, reduce the roll factor to a minimum.

Take the most lofted club in the bag—a sand wedge (if it had a number, it would be around No. 12). Address the ball as in Situation 1A, but a little more to the right, leaving the hand slightly in front of the shaft and ball. Use the single-lever swing, perhaps with a bit of wrist-break on the backswing. Feel your arms leading the club in a sharp downward movement, to get the clubhead under the ball; and to create more backspin through the "tiddlywinks" effect mentioned earlier.

In some situations like this, getting the ball to stop at the desired point means that its first bounce must be short of the green. This is a risk we do not normally want to take, but are forced to face at such times.

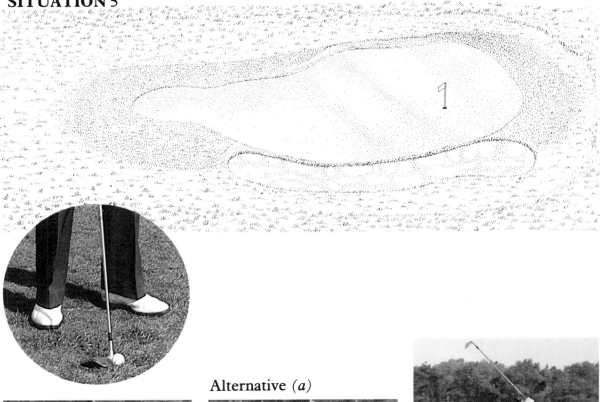

Alternative (a)

Analysis

The ball lies on the fairway, about 20 yards from the front edge of the green and 45 yards from the flag. The flag stands on the right side of the green, close to the sloping edge. The target area is relatively small—and quite firm, as it uaually is on the top section of a plateau green, which drains quickly. The area directly along a line between the ball and flag is clear, but the right side of the green—with its bank, slope, and bunker—lurks dangerously near.

Shot picture

Two alternatives: (a) a high-flying pitch shot directly onto the plateau level, as near the plateau bank as you dare, and on a line

Alternative (b)

going 1 – 2 yards left of the flag;
or (b), a lower flying pitch that bounces on
the lower level of the green and rolls up the
slope to the hole.

Technique/club choice

Alternative (a) demands a high-flying precision shot from 45 – 50 yards. This can be
out of reach for shorter-hitting golfers who
cannot get such distance and accuracy with a
wedge or sand wedge, which are the clubs
required here. For these golfers, alternative
(b) is more reliable.

With alternative (a), the two-lever swing
is needed because:

(1) The length of shot requires sufficient
    speed in the clubhead.

(2) The high-flying shot with stopping force
requires speed in the clubhead to create
immediate backspin on the ball, so that it
can rise quickly and high, then create a
sharp steep fall to pinpoint the target. This
calls for a "cut shot" played with the sand
wedge or pitching wedge.

Address the ball with your hands ahead,
holding the club shaft a little farther down
for better control. Your stance should be
open, with the shoulders and hips aiming a
little to left of the target, the feet closer
together than in a normal shot, and the body
weight evenly distributed. Bend your wrists
early in the backspin, creating a more
straight back-and-upward movement. On
the forward swing, coordinate your hips and
arms, retaining the angle in your wrists, and
cut firmly down on the ball. Because of the
open clubface in relation to the swing line, a
certain amount of left-to-right (clockwise)
sidespin is put on the ball, making it move a
little to the right after the first bounce.

Alternative (b) is for all categories of
players but, as mentioned previously, it is
necessary for shorter players. The choice of
club is individual, but picturing the shot
beforehand will help. The ball will fly lower
than in alternative (a) and run up the slope.
The skilled golfer will probably take a No. 7
or 8 iron, the shorter hitter a No. 6 or 7.

Set up with your hands over the ball,
square stance, and holding down your grip,
more firmly than normal. Swing back as for
a normal shot, suiting the backswing length
to the shot length. Swing through the ball as
usual, allowing your arms to rotate, thereby
keeping the blade square at impact and the
flight low. It is important that the wrists are
not allowed to break in the follow-through,
and the firm grip helps you by keeping the
feeling of the shot in your upper arms.

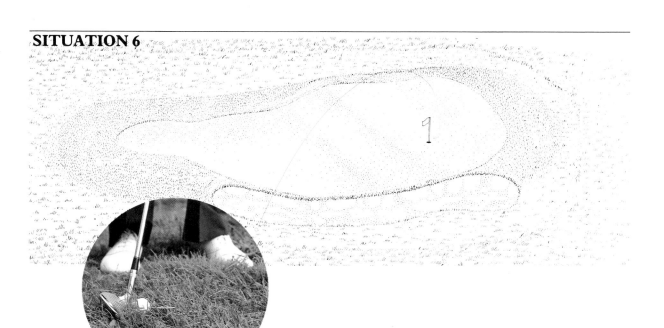

Analysis
The lie of the ball is not good. It rests down in the fairway grass, with rather thick blades just behind the ball. The flag is very close to the near edge of the green, which slopes toward us and down into the bunker that covers most of the area between the ball and flag.

Shot picture
The shot must be as high as possible, to come over the bunker and bounce first on the green. The ball's lie does not help much here, as the grass trapped between blade and ball at impact will greatly reduce the backspin effect. It would be prudent to play tactically and pitch the ball just past the flag, counting on the sloping back of the green to minimize the ball's rolling. The shot can thus be played firmly. In such situations, it is tempting to pitch the ball into the front edge of the green and bounce it up. But since the lie prevents us from exactly knowing the force that will be created at impact, the margin for error is too small and the ball could easily roll back into the bunker. Once again, a longer putt is preferable to a short bunker shot.

Technique/club choice
The "cut shot" played in Situation 5 is the shot for this position. Use the sand wedge, whose wide open blade increases its loft. The force of the shot in the downswing should, because of the resistance from the grass, be greater than what you would normally apply in a shot from that distance.

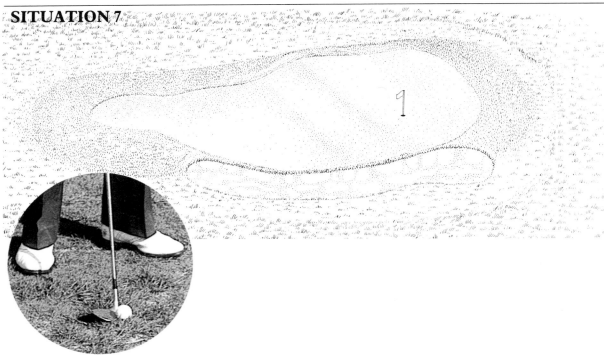

Analysis
A good lie, separated by sand from the flag. This stands on a slope downward from right to left, with a slight uphill slope just short of it.

Shot picture
A high-flying shot, with a soft "drop" up to the flag and a short roll.

Technique/club choice
Set up with the ball forward and your hands slightly behind the ball. Take a wider than normal stance, a little open and with your weight a bit more on the right side. Open the club blade so that it points at the flag. Hold firmly, thereby slowing down the swing. Use a two-lever swing, breaking your wrists quite early on the backswing. Then down, keeping your wrists firm and the blade open. This creates a "lob" shot with some backspin and height due mainly, in this case, to the loft of the club, which is a sand wedge. Don't be tempted to lift the ball with any scooping action—let the clubhead do the work for you.

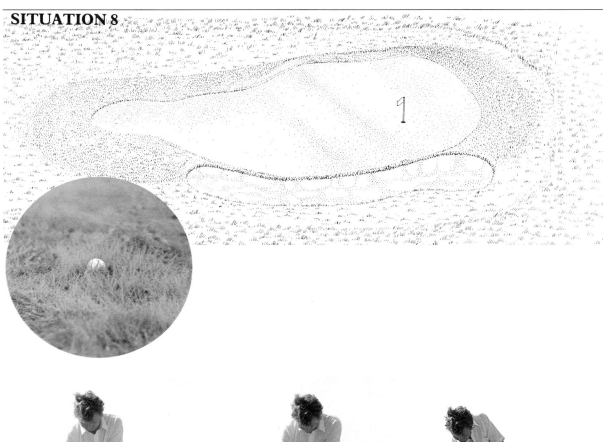

Analysis

The ball lies in the semi-rough and is sitting up on the grass, with "air" under it—about 3 inches to the roots of the grass. Addressing the ball can be a problem, as the ball seems sensitively balanced.

The flag is on the far side of the green, which slopes away down into a bunker behind the hole, as well as down from left to right. The shot must pass 2 – 3 yards of rough, then the fairway and apron which are quite even with no humps. The total length of shot is 15 – 18 yards.

Shot picture

A medium-height pitched shot. Its first bounce is just before the edge of the green, on a line 1.5 yards (1.4 metres) left of the flag. The ball then rolls in from the left and, at worst, stops short of the flag to its right, avoiding an excessive roll and an uphill putt.

Technique/club choice

The ball's lie is an important factor here. It is very easy to go too deeply under the ball, thereby getting a "thin" contact off the top of the club blade, and getting too little power in the shot. The correct club is a No.

91

8 or 9 iron, held firmly down the shaft. A single-lever swing is the simplest method but, if you think there will be a lot of resistance from the grass, a little wrist-action on the backswing is needed to gain clubhead speed.

Chapter 5
IN TROUBLE—AND HOW TO GET OUT

Someone, somewhere has described golf as a game "not so much about hitting perfect shots but more about tidying up after bad ones." Words of wisdom, indeed. The perfect golf round has never been and never will be played. That is one of the beauties of the game. Golf always gives you the opportunity to repair your mistakes, and in that respect it is one of the more human of sports pastimes. My heart goes out to the downhill skier who falls and is out of the competition after a few seconds on the slope. But even if you have a bad start in a golf game, you can still go on to win it. It is human to make mistakes, and it is stimulating to repair what is causing them and then to go on and produce a satisfying result.

Trouble on a golf course can turn up in many guises and is not always the result of a bad shot. A billiards player knows exactly what his playing area looks like, how the balls will react, and so on; it is almost the same for a tennis player, but the golfer is out there competing with Mother Nature and with all the variables that she can produce.

Short shots in sand

In the previous chapter, we touched upon "tidying up" around the greens with chip-ping and pitching shots, so let's continue in the green area with shots from the sand.

If there is one situation that gives the average golfer a feeling of inadequacy, it must be that in which his ball is lying in sand and he has to hit it over the "wall" of the bunker, which is directly in front of a target just a few yards on the other side. But remember, knowledge breeds confidence, and if you can learn the principles behind shots played from the sand, you can turn fear into fun. There are, in fact, several top golfers who, in certain situations, prefer a sand shot to one outside!

The golf swing that you have built up from the beginning is the basis of all two-lever shots, and unless you are going to chip or putt the ball out of the bunker, it is the swing that we are going to use in most of the following situations.

The first thing that you should do when your ball lands in this unusual situation is to build up a feeling of confidence: "I am going to get that ball out of there and into a good position for my next shot!" BUT what most average golfers dare not do is to perform their normal swing while in the "crowded" atmosphere of a bunker. Especially when the shot to be played is only a few yards in total length.

Select a level section of
the bunker and tee a ball
¾ inch above the sand
level. Address the ball as
if you were hitting a shot
from grass. Take a firm

The next step is to make
your own lie in the sand.
Build a little mound,
about ½ inch high. Put a
ball on top. Now, with
the sand wedge and a

stance in the sand,
working your feet down
below the sand level.
This, combined with the
teed-up ball, will mean
that you must hold the
club about 1 inch

further down so that you
do not dig into the sand
behind the ball.

slightly narrower
stance, take some full
swings, and try to take
the sand mound from
under the ball. This
helps you with the new
feeling of hitting

something else than a
ball and to see the ball fly
without having hit it
directly. Do this
without changing your
normal golf swing.

What I would like you to do now is to find
a bunker that allows you to hit some longer
shots. If there is not a bunker in the practice
area with a low enough side, go out and find
one on the course when it is quiet, take a No.
7 iron, a sand wedge, a bucket of practice
balls, and a packet of tees. Try the illustrated exercise.

Your first shots out of the sand will feel as
if you are hitting out of molasses. Your swing
movement will feel restricted. After a while,
however, your normal swing will come
through more and more, and you will begin
to feel at home on sand. It is all a question of
letting your confidence grow.

The displacement of the sand by the clubhead and the sand itself lifts the ball out and
up. The sand also helps to cushion the
power of the swing, helping the ball to come
out softly.

Let's take a break from hitting shots for a
moment and look at the instrument which,
through its design, can cause this effect on
the sand. Let me say immediately that any
golfer who does not have a proper sand club
is seriously limiting his ability to play successful sand shots consistently.

Let's have a look at the club's loft first. A
No. 9 iron has a 48° loft, a pitching wedge
52°, while the average loft of a sand wedge is
56°. Therefore, quickly rising, high shots
are much more difficult to achieve with the
No. 9 iron, and unnecessarily so with the
pitching wedge.

The second thing to consider is the design
of the sole of the sand wedge compared to
that of the other clubs. In order to reduce
the "digging" effect that a normal club has
when entering sand, a good sand wedge has
what is referred to as a bounce sole, which
prevents the digging down and instead

The third step is to place a ball on smooth sand and draw an oval shape around it. The width of the oval should be the same as that of the wedge and its length about 7½ inches, that is 3 inches on either side of the ball.

Now take some shots that try to remove the oval from under the ball, still using the normal swing. The wedge should penetrate the back edge of the oval and continue through the sand, underneath the ball, coming out at the front edge.

To assist you in your assessment and choice of sand wedge, we can refer to the following table from that mine of golf-club information, Ralph Maltby's *Golf Club Design, Fitting, Alteration, and Repair*.

Sand Wedge Selection Table

Width of Sole	Sole Bounce	Swingweight	Loft	Sand Conditions	Performance From Fairway	Comments
Narrow	Slight to Moderate 7° to 11°	Normal D-5 to D-8	56°-60°	Tight, packed sand, not often loosened up and shallow sand. Generally the harder sand type bunkers. Minimum bunker maintenance, rarely raked.	Best — This type sand wedge will work from most all fairway conditions and even from tight lies.	Not good in powdery sand. Fair in loose grainy sand.
Narrow to Medium	Moderate 11° to 14°	Normal to Heavier D-5 to E-0	56°-58°	Loose sand, but very grainy, slight gravel content. Rarely a buried lie. Heavy type sand, large grains, usually dark in color. Moderately raked and maintained.	Good — But bounce can cause problems if fairway conditions are hard with tighter lies.	Works better in powdery sand than in very tight packed sand.
Wide	Moderate to Extreme 12° to 20°	Heavier D-8 to E-2	56°-58°	Powdery, fine texture sand, hand or machine raked often. Buried lies not uncommon. A lot of sand in the traps, usually white in color.	Fair — Not best for fairway shots unless conditions are very plush. A narrower width sole will work better on fairways but with a slight loss in overall sand shot ability unless skill level is high.	Will also work in loose sand but is poorer from tight packed sand.
Medium to Wide	Slight to Moderate 7° to 11°	Normal to Heavier D-5 to E-0	55°-59°	Average sand conditions which vary quite a bit but rarely reach the extremes of tight packed sand or fluffy powdery sand.	Good — Will work from most all fairway conditions but a higher skill level is required on tight lies.	This sand wedge will work in most all types of sand and can be considered a good selection with a minimum of performance tradeoffs.

This chart should be used as a guide only. With all the possible weight, length, sole bounce, sole width, head shape and shaft combinations available in sand wedges today and in the past, it would be all but impossible to accurately describe each sand wedge's playing characteristics.

"slides" through the sand. This helps the player to regulate the amount of sand to be displaced.

The width of the sole has an effect also upon the range of shots that can be played and the type of sand that the club operates in. The wider the sole, the higher the front edge of the club sits off the ground in comparison with a sand wedge that has the same sole arch but a narrower width.

Also, if the clubface is held in an open position, the club that has a wider sole will sit proportionally higher off the ground with its leading edge than one that has a narrow sole.

As we are limited to a maximum of fourteen clubs to be used during a golf round, it is important to select your clubs correctly, so that, where possible, clubs can "double up" in different situations. Choosing a sand wedge that one can use outside of sand areas is desirable, for example when playing higher, shorter shots (covered in the previous chapter), and even when playing from deep rough (see later in this chapter).

The standard sand shots
1. Not too wide a stance. Ball position as with a standard iron shot, slightly to the left of the swing center point.
2. Club shaft vertical with the clubhead above the point where you will penetrate the sand. (It is a two-stroke penalty if you touch the sand with the club at any place before actually making the stroke.)
3. Knees flexed ready for action, with the body weight slightly favoring the left side.
4. The left arm/hand is going to dominate the swing with the right playing its usual supporting role.
5. Leg action on the backswing is minimal, but feel a coordination on the forward swing between the left side and the forward movement of the knees, allowing the left arm/side to be in command all the time. The weight shift towards the left at the knees helps to avoid the flub that the inexperienced player often gets by being too keen to get at the ball with the right hand.
6. Regulate the shot's length by varying the swing tempo. Longer shots, harder swing; shorter shots, easier swing. Keep a reasonably long swing to promote tempo control.
7. Swing through exactly as if it were a normal golf shot.

A good sand wedge has a flange, also referred to as a bounce sole. The object of this flange is to prevent the clubhead from digging down into the sand. The sand

The standard sand shot

So far you have used your normal golf swing when playing bunker shots in order to keep things simple and to help yourself to lose any respect you had for bunkers. You have experienced hitting sand instead of the ball and noted that when the clubhead has come properly in the sand under the ball, the sand becomes your ally and forces the ball upwards and forwards.

Let us summarize the swing fundamentals in relation to the standard sand shot from a good lie:

wedge can be used for non-sand shots, too, for example for green-approach shots that must come in high to avoid hazards around the green.

Some situations that require some variations to our standard swing.

1. The ball is lying down in the sand: a "half-good lie"

If we use our standard swing, we will get a thin strike, because the standard swing is a sweeping movement that creates a sort of 'U'-shaped arc through the sand under the ball.

To get the ball to lift from this lie, the clubhead must come deeper under the ball.

This we can do by having the ball more to the right at the start position, a maximum of one golf ball's size, and by moving the hands further forward (to-wards the target) so that they are in line with the front of the ball.

This will create a steeper up-and-down swing that causes the clubhead to go deeper into the sand under the ball. The shape of this swing can be said to resemble the letter 'V'.

2. The ball lies deep in the sand: a bad lie

Close the blade as much as you judge fit, taking into account sand texture and your own strength. The harder the swing needed, the deeper your feet should be in the sand, thus lowering your swing.

As soon as you start the backswing, break your wrists. For once, you may chop your swing.

This is a difficult situation that involves the rules of golf as well as the swing technique. See the separate box on the next page.

As with every trouble situation, time taken to think through your position is time well spent. For instance, if a lie is deep in sand, a few seconds' logical thought will make it clear that, in order to get the ball to fly, the clubhead must come deep under the ball. This forces both sand and ball upwards. For this to happen, the clubhead must penetrate the sand behind the ball with a steep angle of attack.

A little more thought will indicate that the clubhead is in the sand for a longer time and that the resisting pressure exerted on the club face will have a tendency to turn the blade around the shaft, i.e., it will open it. How much the blade opens depends on the amount of resistance offered by the sand, the counter-resistance from the hands and arms, and the blade-closing swing action of the player.

Finally, you will be able to deduce that as there will be a fair amount of sand between the club blade and the ball, there is going to be less backspin and this will result in some roll when the ball hits the ground.

1. You are not allowed to move the sand around the ball in order to identify it, but there is no penalty if, after playing the shot, you discover that the ball was not yours.
2. If the lie is hopeless, the rules help you out with the "unplayable lie" rule. This gives the bunkered player two alternatives:
(*a*) Return to the position from which you hit the shot that landed you in the unplayable lie, drop a ball within two club lengths of that position, and take a penalty stroke.
(*b*) Drop a ball within two club lengths from the unplayable lie, not closer to the hole and within the bunker, and take a penalty of one stroke.

So you see, you can "buy" yourself out of tough situations quite cheaply: only one stroke is added to the score. This is definitely worth considering in difficult situations.

What now can we conclude from the above analysis?
1. During the backswing, the wrists must break earlier than usual in order to create the necessary sharp angle of descent in the downswing (a very 'V'-formed swing).
2. You must make allowance for the blade opening, and this depends on your strength and on the texture of the sand.
3. When you are planning the strength of your swing in relation to the finished shot, you must take ball roll into account, and this will also depend on the resistance offered by the surface of the ground.

Judge the sand
Sand can vary in type from course to course. What interests you about the sand is (*a*) the amount of resistance it will make to the swinging golf club, and (*b*) the depth of raked sand in the bunker. The more airy, or "fluffy," the sand, the less force is needed from the club head. Coarse tightly packed sand needs more force. This you vary by the tempo of the swing. When playing away from your home course, you may have to regulate your swing to suit the different sand conditions; you must "add on" or "take away" power from your "home course" swing.

Wet sand creates a cement-type of consistency and resistance, so on wet sand you are going to need a sharper downswing (of the 'V' type) with the clubhead square or even a little closed, for better sand penetration.

Note: When you are addressing the ball, check with your feet if the sand under the surface is wet or dry—this is important when the ball lies down in the sand.

Long shots from sand

Although the majority of sand bunkers are situated around the greens, golf-course architects use sand to "toughen up" a golf hole at other places, either to steer play in a certain direction, to penalize a bad drive, or sometimes even to prevent a ball rolling unfairly into water or out of bounds.

Generally speaking, the further the bunker is from the green, the lower the front side is. On some of the elder links courses in Scotland, one can find really deep fairway bunkers that even have steps down into them! The player is often forced to play a shot out sideways or even backwards, away from the green. But, as I said, most fairway bunkers are designed to penalize a wayward shot and to test the player's skill at the "repair" shot.

Nearly all trouble shots are a mixture of technique and tactics. Your basic philosophy in dealing with trouble should be to move, with the minimum of risk, the ball as close to the hole as possible and to a position from where you can play the simplest possible shot.

The first thing you do upon arriving at your ball is to check the lie, because this decides to a great extent the choice of club.

If the lie is good, i.e., the ball is lying level on top of the sand, with the striking side of the ball free from sand, then, from the point

1. A good lie in sand.
The ball is lying on top
of the sand, level, and
there is lots of space to
the front of the bunker.
A wood can be used
here.

2. A half-good lie fairly
near the front of the
bunker. Iron No.7, 8, or
9 should lift the ball out
nicely with reasonable
length.

3. A bad lie, deep in the
sand and perilously near
the front. The sand
wedge is the only choice
here.

of view of the ball's lie, there is no limit to
the club choice. If the ball is lying down in
the sand or on a sloping part of the bunker,
then our choice of club is limited. As we
shall look at shots played from uneven lies
on the course later on, we need only discuss
the ball lie in the sand just now.

From a "half-good" lie, both distance and
height of shot are severely restricted because the sand will almost certainly come
the club blade and the ball at impact. Only
the more lofted irons, Nos. 8, 9, and the
pitching wedge, are available to us in such
situations. (We must bear in mind that our
primary goal is to hit the next shot from a
reasonably normal lie, i.e., not from the
same bunker!).

In deep sand lies, only the sand wedge
should be considered, but extra thought
must be given to direction, as the length of

the shot will be severely limited. In extreme
cases, this may mean taking the nearest way
out of the bunker, even if that way is away
from the flag. Swing technique for these bad
lies is the same as that for lies in greenside
bunkers.

If the lie in the bunker is good, then the
choice of club should be affected by the
following factors:
(a) The distance to the hole.
(b) The distance from the ball to the edge of
the bunker over which you have to lift
the ball.
(c) The height of that bunker edge.
(d) The target area for the shot, resulting
from your analysis of the preceding
three factors.
(e) Club-blade loft reduction, due to the
adjustment in your swing technique (see
page 99).

Shot technique adjustments

Adjustment No. 1: The feet

Hitting a long shot from sand will often feel a little strange because you are standing on relatively unstable ground while taking a full swing. So you must establish a firm base for your swing.

The problem areas are on the outsides of both feet. When you swing the club back, the body weight shifts to the right, putting extra pressure on the supporting right foot. On sand, this can cause the right foot to slide "open" to the right, resulting in too much body movement in that direction and increasing the risk of striking the sand behind the ball.

On the forward swing, you have the same problem with the left foot, resulting in too much swing movement to the left, which causes a thin or topped shot.

The remedy for this is to pull the knees towards each other when addressing the ball. This pushes the insides of the feet down into the sand to build up a kind of platform under the outsides of the feet. This platform will help prevent unwanted sideways body movement during the swing.

Adjustment No. 2: Ball to the right at address

Probably the most frustrating shot in golf is called the "flub," i.e., when you hit the ground instead of the ball. If this happens when you are playing from sand, the result is a catastrophe because the sand kills the clubhead speed very quickly and little shot distance is obtained.

To reduce the possibility of a duff, I recommend that you take your address position with the ball about half a golf-ball size more to the right than you would have for a shot of the same distance played from the fairway. This means that, at address, the club blade's effective loft will be reduced slightly (probably by up to one club number difference). Remember, however, to take this adjustment into consideration when choosing the right club for each fairway-bunker situation.

Practice from a fairway bunker will teach

(Left) Work your feet down into the sand to give firm footing for good balance. Then pull your knees towards each other, pushing down some more with the insides of your feet. The platforms of sand that you now build up under the outsides of both feet will help stop sideways body movement during the swing.

Have the ball slightly more to the right than you would if addressing a shot of the same distance on the fairway. This will reduce the loft of your club slightly, giving the ball a lower trajectory and longer flight.

you how the ball will fly when struck with different clubs, and in order to choose the right club you must know how quickly the ball will rise when struck with the different lofts.

Try to avoid using a club that, with a perfect stroke, will only just get the ball over the edge of the bunker. Give yourself a good margin for error. It is better to finish short of the target than risk driving the ball into an unplayable lie in the face of the bunker.

Shots from uneven lies

The very nature of the golf game ensures that we are continuously provided with new challenges. Golf is not a fair game. Good golf shots can finish in unfair lies. You may try to plan your game according to the terrain, but often you must accept—even plan—that the ball is going to finish in a position other than the standard one from which we practice most, i.e., the flat lie with the ball and player on the same level.

Adapting to the different lie levels is not difficult but, like everything else, requires routine and practice.

1. A sidehill lie where the ball is above the level of the feet

(*Center*) With the ball higher than the feet, a correctly soled golf blade points to the left of the target.

(*Right*) Adopt a balanced start position (feet a little farther from the ball and weight more toward toes). Aim to the right of the target.

The first time you encounter this kind of situation, you will probably take a large portion of God's earth and the ball, if it moves at all, will curve to the left of the target.

The address position will feel "crowded," but don't worry about this, because after all, the ball is closer than normal to you and to your golf swing's center point. Instinctively, you are going to feel that you want to stand more upright from the waist upwards to create more space for the swing. To do this a little is correct and natural.

But even this will not prevent the club from digging into the ground behind the ball if the slope is rather steep. What we must do is to shorten the distance from the clubhead to the center point of the swing by quite simply gripping lower down on the club. How much further down? That depends, of course, upon the severity of the slope. Find this out by taking some practice swings close by from a similar position. You should be satisfied only when the clubhead brushes the ground where the ball will lie. These address position adjustments will give correct ball contact.

Now, as regards the flight direction of the shot, the ball will tend to curve to the left. This is due mainly to the fact that the clubhead, when soled correctly (flush with the sloping ground) at address, is pointing to the left of the ball-to-target line. *As the chosen club's loft increases, so does the number of degrees the blade points left.* This "closed" club-blade position puts a right-to-left sidespin on the ball and, if you are using one of the shorter irons, it can even *start* the ball flight to the left.

The simplest way out of this situation is to align yourself to the right of the target and swing normally, allowing the club-blade position at impact to swing the ball back onto the target. Don't forget, though, that a closed-blade position at impact reduces the effective loft of the blade and thereby the height of the shot. Note also that holding further down the grip at address shortens the swing radius, thus giving a somewhat lower clubhead speed. This will normally reduce shot length, but this could be compensated by the previously noted reduced loft position.

2. A sidehill lie where the ball is lower than the level of the feet

(Center) With the ball lower than the feet, there is a tendency for the blade to aim a little right of target.

(Right) A centralized body weight distribution at address is important for keeping balance during the swing.

A low thinned or topped shot is the most common from a lie where the ball is lower than the level of the feet. The problem here is exactly the opposite of the previous one, as the distance between the ball and the swing center point is greater than normal. Instinctively, you try to lengthen the club in some way, for instance by holding it further up the grip. This is not to be recommended, as you then lose control of the club. So what do you do? Well, if you cannot move the ball closer to the center point of the swing, then you must move the center point closer to the ball. There are two steps in this shot technique adjustment.

1. Bend more at the knees. This lowers the swing center point. Basically, what you do is to adopt an exaggerated sitting position at address.

2. Exaggerate the forward bend from the hips, making sure that you adjust your body weight to keep the balance centered over the balls of your feet. (This will also help keep the sole of the club nearer to the normal flush-to-the-ground position.)

On severe slopes, the use of the shorter irons can provide you with a problem, due to their more upright "lie" (the angle between the shaft and the clubhead sole). The solution here is to hold as far down the grip as is comfortable while standing to the ball and to address it with the ball as close to the heel of the club as possible.

Another solution to the steep-slope lie is to use a wooden club instead of a longer iron, as the wooden club's "lie" is flatter than that of the iron, and this provides a more correct clubhead position behind the ball. If you need to reduce the length of the shot with the wood, you can hold it further down the grip, thereby reducing clubhead swing speed.

From this sidehill lie, there can be a tendency to fade the ball (i.e., to the right). Note how much this fade is when you use different clubs, either during practice or when playing. The adjustment you then need to make is to set up the appropriate amount to the left of the target, allowing the ball to curve back to the target.

3. An uphill lie

This is the easiest of the sloping lies, but nevertheless some preparation adjustments have to be made.

There are two mistakes that can be made from this lie. Either the ball is struck thinly and flies lower than normal, or it is struck well but flies too high and short.

The thinned or even topped shot is a result of the ball being struck before the clubhead reaches the ground. In other words, it is struck too early in the forward swing, and this is due to the slope. The adjustment is to address the ball where the club reaches the ground, and in the case of the uphill lie, this is more to the left (i.e., nearer the higher placed foot).

The high-trajectory shot comes from the fact that you are hitting the ball with an upward-moving swing—upward as compared to horizontal. This is caused by the fact that, very naturally, you are standing into the slope at address, in order to be able to hold your balance during the swing. This gives the forward swing into the ball too steep an angle of approach when the angle of the slope is considered. To correct this, lean to the right with the upper body so that it is as close to 90° with the slope as possible, while still retaining comfort and balance for most of the swing back and through the ball.

Summary
1. Ball more to the left at address.
2. Choose a less lofted club, to lessen the effect of the abnormally high ball trajectory.
3. Keep the upper body as close to an angle of 90° to the slope as your swing balance will permit.

On an uphill lie, you should try to keep your shoulder line parallel to the slope, without, of course, jeopardizing your balance. This helps keep the swing arc of the clubhead following the slope so that it contacts the back of the ball solidly.

In uphill and downhill lie situations, have the ball positioned nearest the highest foot. In the downhill lie shown, this means the right foot.

As with the uphill lie, the tendency is for the body to lean into the slope at address. And the remedy is, again, to position the upper body to the left as much as is comfortable and as near to 90° to the slope as possible.

As mentioned, the ball will fly lower than normal, so club selection is important. Bear in mind that a more lofted club is shorter in shaft, and even though the desired shot trajectory be attained, the clubhead speed will be lower and the shot shorter. For instance, if the length and the trajectory required are those normally given by a No. 5 iron on a level lie, a No. 6 iron may produce the same trajectory (depending, of course, on the angle of slope), but as the No. 6 iron is ½ inch shorter than the No. 5, the clubhead speed will be slightly lower, producing a shorter shot.

The simplest way to make up for this length deficit is to increase the swing tempo. Make sure, however, that you can control the extra speed. A wider stance will help you to do this.

Pitching or playing sand shots from downhill lies close to the green can be a problem, due to the lower trajectory and the consequent difficulty in pinpointing the target. An open stance (to the left) coupled with the extra loft gained from an open club blade at address can produce the required height.

The ball lying on the downhill slope presents the more difficult of the slope situations, because the ball will fly lower than normal in comparison to a ball struck with the same club from the level. The problem is exacerbated if you are near the green and want the ball to stop or want to lift the ball over something.

The wrong stroke here can result in your hitting the ground behind the ball. The ground to the right of the ball on a downhill slope is higher than that to the left. This means that on the forward swing the clubhead contacts the ground earlier than it would if the lie were level. So you must have the ball lying nearer the highest foot, the right.

Summary
1. Ball more to the right at address.
2. Upper body 90° to the slope.
3. Select a more lofted club and use, if required, a higher swing tempo to achieve the same length of shot.
4. With a shorter pitch or sand shot, use an open stance and open club blade at address. You have probably noticed one common factor in all the four lies discussed here: the upper body at address is positioned as close as swing balance will allow, to a 90-degree-to-the-slope angle. This is to make the swing with the arm and club around the center point follow the ground in the same way as if the ball lay on the level.

Good lie in the rough. You can get at the ball with a wood.

Half-good lie. Club selection rather limited to maximum No. 6 iron.

Bad lie. The heavy, lofted sand wedge is your best bet here (if you opt to play the ball).

Shots from the rough

"Rough" is the name given to the longer grass found off the fairway. The lie of the ball in the rough will dictate the swing technique you will use. So it is not until you get to the ball and see how it is sitting that your shot planning can start.

As we did when discussing the short game in Chapter 4, we will divide the lie of the ball into three categories: good, half-good, and bad.

Good lies

If you are fortunate after hitting the ball into the rough, you can find it sitting up in the grass almost as if it were teed up. This occurs often on courses in warmer climates where the grass is strong and can hold the weight of the ball. In such a situation, you can play the same club that you would use from the fairway. But if there is some grass behind the ball, which can be trapped between the blade and ball at impact, a "flier" can result. (A flier is a shot that flies lower and longer than normal, because of the reduced grip effect between club blade and ball and the subsequent backspin given to the ball by the club blade). If you suspect that you might get a flier, use a more lofted club, for instance a No. 6 instead of a No. 4, to compensate for this extra length.

(*Note:* This situation is not limited to the rough but can arise on any good lie where grass can come between the ball and the club blade.)

When addressing a ball in this "teed-up" lie in the rough, be careful that you do not hit it, or you will be penalized one stroke. I would, therefore, recommend you to hold the clubhead slightly over the grass behind the ball. In extreme "teed-up" situations, hold the club a little further down the grip. Position yourself so that the ball is one golf-ball size more to the right than normal. This encourages a slightly more downward stroke on the ball, thereby making sure the ball flies quickly up and out.

As mentioned, you can take whichever club you feel you need for the distance, although I would suggest that the high-handicap player play the longer shots with the No. 5 wood.

Summary

1. Check the lie of the ball. Is it a possible "flier"?
2. Hold the clubhead over the grass at address, and maybe hold it further down the grip.
3. At address, the ball should be one golf-ball size more to the right.
4. Swing normally.

Grass behind the ball can reduce clubhead speed, while rough in front will be in the ball's flight path.

Half-good lies

The first and most important thing you must do when you find your ball in a lie that is not good is to form a realistic picture of the flight of the shot *from that lie*. In these situations, our inexperienced golfer will lose shots because he or she will attempt that "dream shot" that comes only once in every hundred attempts. After all, it does not help much to be able to talk about that miracle shot on the fourth hole if the ball flew farther than planned and into even more trouble!

Top golfers do not rely on miracles. They plan after known facts and their own hard-earned experience. They know that most of your shots from half-good lies will be reduced in length and probably wayward in direction. Remember that realistic planning in all trouble situations is a major part of the successfully produced shot.

When you come up to the ball in the rough, check the following:
1. The distance from the ball to the flag.

2. The amount of resistance that the grass behind the ball will give the clubhead.
3. The amount of resistance that the grass in front of the ball will give to the ball after impact.

The facts that you gather from these observations, together with what you know about your own golf swing, will enable you to decide which club is required to get the ball as close to the hole as possible.

If you decide that you cannot reach the green, then you must establish a new target *with a good margin for error in both length and direction*. This is important because the control of this shot is greatly reduced, and the last thing you want to end up with is more trouble somewhere else. At this stage, it is better to plan taking an extra shot to put yourself into a more normal shot situation in which you will have more to say about how the ball will fly.

So, establish a large target area and choose your club. The chances are that the least lofted club you can with certainty take will be about a No. 6 or No. 7 iron.

Address the ball with the club blade open and the ball positioned as with the good lie, a little to the right. The blade must be open because, in this longer-grass situation, the grass will wrap around the shaft as the club travels through the rough towards the ball. This creates a braking effect in the shaft area and causes the club blade to rotate (to close) around the shaft. When playing from very wiry grass or from a heavy lie, this closing effect can be accentuated and the result must, therefore, be built into the planned golf shot.

Summary
1. After the lie inspection:
  (a) visualize the finished shot;
  (b) choose the target area;
  (c) choose the club.
2. Open the club blade according to the judged strength of the grass or other rough.
3. Position the body with the ball more to the right.
4. Use the normal swing.

Bad lies

There are similarities from lies in the deep rough and bad lies in the sand. First, you can decide to play the ball or use the "un-playable lie" rule. The two "drop" alternatives discussed earlier (*see page 100*) are still available, but now that you are outside the bunker, there is a third possibility.

Should you decide to play the shot, the swing adjustments to be applied are the same as for a bad lie in sand, with the exception that the club blade must be *open* at address, for the reason mentioned in the

In deep-rough situations, hold firmly with blade open.

Stand firmly, a little wider than normal, with a locked feeling at the knees.

The V-shaped swing used in buried sand lies is ideal for deep-rough positions. Chop sharply down into the back of the ball with the *intention* of a large follow through.

You may drop the ball behind the point where the ball lay, keeping that point between yourself and the hole, with no limit to how far behind that point the ball may be dropped. One penalty stroke is to be added to the score for the hole.

So thought no. 1 is, "Can I win anything by playing this shot or is it better to use the unplayable-ball rule alternatives?" Don't be too proud to use the rules—they were created to help you on your voyage through the eighteen holes of God's nature. One stroke in penalty is a very cheap way of "buying" yourself out of trouble.

"half-good lie" plus the fact that you increased the club's loft when opening the blade.

In these deeper lies, the club most often used is the sand wedge. Besides being the most lofted club, it is the heaviest, and therefore gives the club the most force when it encounters heavy vegetation.

A harder swing than normal is required here, so you need a wider stance to provide stability. Once again, the ball should be a little to the right of standard at address. And you must make the same swing adjustment as you did in the sand lie: the wrist must bend immediately on the backswing, thus creating a sharp upright movement with a resulting "chopping" down and forward swing. It is imperative to keep the arms leading in this downward movement in order to keep the clubhead moving down and *in* under the ball, taking the grass or whatever is underneath.

It may be that the resistance from the vegetation is so great that a follow-through movement is limited. This does not matter so much, as the important thing is that the sharp downswing should avoid, as much as possible, collecting rough between the club blade and the ball, and thereby deliver maximum power to the back and underside of the ball.

Obviously, length of shot is going to be limited. Indeed, in these situations you are often quite happy to see the ball move only a few yards, *but it must be a worthwhile distance and to a better line to the target or to a better lie* or you may as well have played the ball under the unplayable-ball rule. Don't be greedy about length; if you are close to the fairway, aim for that, even if it means playing sideways or back away from the green.

Summary

1. Establish a realistic target area and ask yourself if you can win anything by playing the ball as it lies. The alternative is a drop.
2. If you choose a sand wedge, open the blade. Ball to the right of standard at address, and a wide stance.
3. Break the wrists sharply on the backswing, chopping down into the back and *underside* of the ball.

Chapter 6
YOUR GOLF ROUND

Thus far, we have concentrated on helping you develop a basic repertoire of golf shots to get you around the course with the least amount of pain. Diligent practice, with the accent upon quality of shots rather than quantity, should after a while begin to give you a reasonable success standard.

It is important to realize that no one has ever mastered golf completely. Jack Nicklaus reckons to hit about ten to fifteen per cent of his shots exactly as planned. It is fun to hit a perfect shot, but it is as much fun, if not more, to be able to repair a situation and still make the planned score for the whole.

This chapter and the next are concerned with our conduct on the course, from planning our round, analyzing the results, checking development, getting to know ourselves, and influencing our attitudes to the game through relaxation exercises. Some of what we are going to discuss now may seem far removed from where you are in the development of your game. You may feel that the most important just now is to improve your shot techniques, but very early in your development, you will come to the stage where the number of shots you take around the course is all-important.

Course management

The planning of your game and the matching of your skills to the course is commonly referred to as course management. In course management, you combine three different types of golfing skill: technical, mental, and physical. When you stand on the first tee, prior to an 18-hole golf round, you are equipped with a certain amount of these three skills, which are your strength, your "plus" qualities. It is these strengths that you use to match yourself to the course.

An example of a "strength" from my own game is that, with the woods and longer irons (Nos. 2, 3, and 4), I expect the shot to fade somewhat. Funny kind of strength, you might say, but not really, because this is a shape of shot that *I can rely on*. Because of this, I now try, as often as I can, to plan my golf around this strength.

Another example of a strength is my preference for chipping rather than pitching, so that when I am confronted with a long shot onto the green, I plan the shot so that, if I do not hit the green, I am left with a chip rather than a pitch.

Now I can just hear you saying that this is all right for someone who has achieved a high

This faded approach shot leaves an easy chip onto the green, which suits me perfectly. If my shot had been drawn, it would have landed on the wrong side of the bunker, leaving me with a pitch.

standard of control over his shots and can plan his game accordingly. But my point is that *all* golfers have "strengths," according to the stage they are at in their development. It is with knowing these strengths (and weaknesses) that our first step towards successful play on the course is concerned.

Defining your present playing profile

We have broadly defined the skills required as being technical, mental, and physical. Over the years, golf has gained the undeserved image of being only a game and not a sport. Golf is, of course, what you want it to be, but even if your aims stay at the weekend recreation level, you soon discover that success in shotmaking is affected by your physical and mental qualities. Hitting golf shots on the practice area is one thing, but a successful shot in a last-hole, "chance to win" situation requires more than just a sound technique.

If you have just started to play the game, then shot technique is of prime importance. Some areas of your game will develop more quickly than others, and, for a certain period, you will find your game in a constantly changing state. During this period, it is difficult to plan a round of golf, but after some time your game will acquire a certain stability, and you can begin to establish your playing profile. This is nothing more complicated than a summary of the "cans" and

"can'ts" of your present strengths and weaknesses. This can be done by analyzing your round-summary records.

"Now hold on there," I can hear you saying. "I'm only out for a little exercise and recreation, I don't want to win the Open Championship! I have enough paperwork in my job!" Well, it is my contention (and experience) that most people who spend about four hours per round on a golf course, as well as some time on practice, want to improve. It is more fun to be able to play better golf; you get more out of playing different courses and competing with better

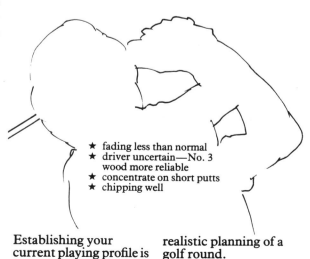

★ fading less than normal
★ driver uncertain—No. 3 wood more reliable
★ concentrate on short putts
★ chipping well

Establishing your current playing profile is paramount to the realistic planning of a golf round.

players if you get as close as you can to your maximum performance potential. If nothing else, normal human curiosity to see how good one can be is a common driving force.

A golf-round summary and the subsequent analysis form the base for your play, practice sessions, and skill development. The analysis helps give a picture of you—the golf player.

Golf-round Summary	No. of shots	Comments
Tee and transport shots including par 3 holes		
Target area hits	10	Two were thinned
Target area misses—left	1	Pulled
Target area misses—right	7	Five slices, two pushes
Green hits within the intended sector	8	Three rather thinned
Green misses—left	5	All pulls (one from sidehill lie)
Green misses—right	0	
Green misses—short	4	Two thinned shots. Two wrong club choice
Green misses—long	1	Wrong club
Short Game		
Chip shots to within 1 yard of hole	5	Feels OK. Control is good
Chip shots outside 1 yard of hole	0	
From max 50 yards		
Pitch shots to within 5 yards of hole	0	
Pitch shots outside 5 yards of hole	3	All to left. Too far from hole
From Greenside bunker		
Sand shot to within 2 yards of hole	0	
Sand shot outside 2 yards of hole	2	Short both times. Too much sand
Putting		
Three-putts below 10 yards of hole	4	1 long downhill. Three were straight but short

Any part of your game can be charted this way. Say that a fault of yours is slicing and that you are working on improving this. You can keep track of your progress during, say, ten rounds, by plotting a chart like this, with the score in blue and faults in red.

In the first game, your score was 20 above par and your fault frequency was 8 (i.e., you sliced eight times). After the ten rounds (and the practice sessions in between each round), your score is 10 above par and your slice frequency is 4.

It is interesting to note that, during the first five games, your fault frequency actually rose. Your conscious efforts to improve had not worked its way into your subconscious, so you were too tense. The score got worse in the early games, too, before improving steadily.

Now it is back to round analysis again, to pinpoint other weak areas in your game, a new improvement development plan, and a new progress chart to provide the encouragement.

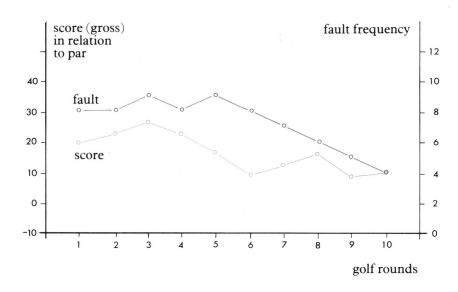

This round analysis lists the major areas of the game that require technical skill. These, of course, can be broken down into a more detailed description, if such information is required. For example, the lie of the ball can be built into our commentary column as an explanation for an errant shot. Shots from roughs and fairway bunkers could also be added to the major headings.

As it stands, the analysis informs you of your playing tendencies, and this is necessary information when planning for improvement. For example, a good teaching professional will require a true picture of what you do on the course in order to be able to help you effectively on the lesson tee. And another thing, the valuable spare time you spend practicing should be concentrated on improving your *known* weaknesses (while, of course, keeping up the best parts of your game). It is important that you can glean the desired information from the analysis chart. For example, the chart might tell you that you are taking too many putts. Putting improvement can, of course, help, but a closer look behind the scores could reveal that the shots played to the green are seldom close enough to the flag, thereby placing too much pressure on putting skills. An ever deeper examination of your play could indicate poor strategy from the tee, or that the longer "transport" shots leave very difficult approach shots to the green, resulting in too many long-putt situations.

The ambitious golfer can now, having identified the weaker parts of his or her game, decide upon an improvement plan and keep a check on his or her development through progress charts of the kind shown here.

When you feel that your shot technique has reached a stable level, then probably further shot and score improvement can come as a result of taking a look "behind the scenes," or checking on your mental skills. In other words, you might consider that some of your bad shots are not due to faulty technique but are caused further behind the scenes by some unwanted mental activity. For example, a player who has been controlling the ball well for most of the round, suddenly, on the seventeenth tee, slices out of bounds. He could possibly have been intimidated by, for example, his match or score status or, quite simply, by a mental picture of his ball flying out of bounds. If that player comes off the eighteenth green with the impression that he has a technique fault in the form of a slice, and spends time and money in working on this, he may just be missing the true reason for that slice (and probably for other bad shots). Such mental round analysis demands complete self-honesty but can lead to more effective golf training (and possibly to benefits in your personal life, too!).

Planning and playing

"Beauty is in the eye of the beholder," runs the expression. Certainly, appreciation of a golf course is quite individual. There was a time, it is said, when Lee Trevino, one of golf's all-time greats, refused to play in the prestigious Masters tournament at Augusta National, Georgia, because of the design of the course. This did not mean that Trevino could not appreciate the subtlety of the layout or the magnificent natural surroundings. It was just the fact that Trevino's natural shape of shot, a fade, did not fit the design of the course, which contains many dogleg-left holes. In recent years, Trevino has come to terms with Augusta and is a more complete golfer for it.

Trevino's experience reminds us of an ancient law of golf: "Play the ball as it lies and the course as it is." Over the years, the rules of golf have been developed to assist us in unfair situations as regards lie of ball and condition of course, but the acceptance of the course as designed and of the resulting play situations is a fact of golfing life. Due to seasonal and even daily weather conditions, a golf course is a continually changing challenge and, in order to be able to meet this challenge, an analysis of the "course of the day" is necessary. In actual fact, the match is *"you-today"* versus *"the course today."*

Determining *your* pre-round status is the first step in planning your journey around the course. This is one of the more important reasons for hitting a certain number of shots on the practice area prior to play. After fifteen to twenty loosening-up shots, you will be in a position to establish a preliminary "picture" of how you and your golf swing are performing. The next twenty to twenty-five shots should be observed carefully and the flight tendency noted, because it is this shot profile together with your previous experience that will form the basis of your *round plan*.

Why plan?
Being able to plan a round of golf beforehand sounds, of course, a bit naive and rather like wonderland, but compiling your own "road-map" has several advantages.

First. It revises constantly your own playing capability, which will keep you up to date with your current status, thereby helping you to plan how to improve.

Second. It makes you perform a mental "dress-rehearsal" of the round, thereby helping to create a more relaxed "at-home" state of mind for the actual round.

Third. It helps you avoid the "I always hit a 5-iron here" way of thinking; you are matching "you as you are *now*" to "the situation *now*".

Fourth. A round plan helps keep you on the rails. Let me explain. Suppose that your playing plan for the first four holes gives you a 5, 4, 5, 5 start, and you start 4, 3, 4, 4. Four strokes better than calculated. What

115

Have a pre-round plan for your "journey" round the course. This will keep your whole round "on the rails" despite unexpected happenings.

sort of thoughts begin to fly around in your head? "Reduced handicap, winning the competition, personal best score," and so on. Having a round plan keeps your feet on the ground and enables you to concentrate on the job in hand, which is the next shot and hole. By the same token, a catastrophic snow-ball effect that can occur after a bad hole, or holes, can be avoided because you are so engaged in carrying out your plans that what has happened, both good and bad, is more easily put behind you.

Fifth. Your round plan helps keep you from trying to hit "one-out-of-a-hundred" dream shots. You plan according to your resources today, not your dreams for tomorrow!

Sixth. The round plan and the subsequent comparison with the actual result gives you a more realistic picture of your golfing capability, and this in turn can help avoid the disappointment that often accompanies unrealistic expectations.

Seventh. You notice more about yourself and the golf course—you observe more, experience more, and this must surely increase your sense of fulfilment at playing the game better.

If by now I have succeeded in convincing you that there might lie something productive in this planning business then I would like us to take a more detailed look.

Shot distance

In order to be able to plan your golf rounds properly and to clear up your mistakes effectively, you must get to know how far you hit the ball with the different clubs. Through practice and play, the number of strikes you will make that are "on-center," that is, the center of the ball is in line with the sweetspot of the clubface, will increase, and assuming that your swing tempo has also stabilized itself, you will achieve a more reliable shot length with the different clubs.

Now, although one of our dreams with golf is to perfect our striking, human fallibility sometimes has its say, and variation in striking and consequently in length will occur. One of the average golfer's major faults is that he or she expects and plans for a perfect contact between club and ball, in other words maximum length of shot.

One of the first facts of golfing life we must accept is that there is going to be variation in this contact position and that we must base our round plan on our *average* length shot with each number of club. This average is the middle distance between our best and our not-so-good strikes. Obvious-

ly, we cannot base our calculation on our absolutely worst shots but it is possible to establish a reliable, average length. This can be done either in yards or in paces. That is to say, you must know on average how far you hit with each of the clubs in your bag, measured in yards or normal walking paces. Many courses these days have some sort of distance marker 150 yards from the center of the green. This measured distance can assist you in establishing your shot distance.

One quiet and windless day, walk this 150 yards and note the number of paces you take. Then go to the practice range, choose a level area, and select twenty to twenty-five balls of good condition, and number them. Having warmed up, hit the No. 5-iron shots at the target, noting as you play the numbers of the balls that you feel were not representative of your present striking standard. Upon completion, take these balls away. You now have left a pattern of shots from which to establish

(a) the average distance of the shots played,
(b) a representative maximum and minimum length.

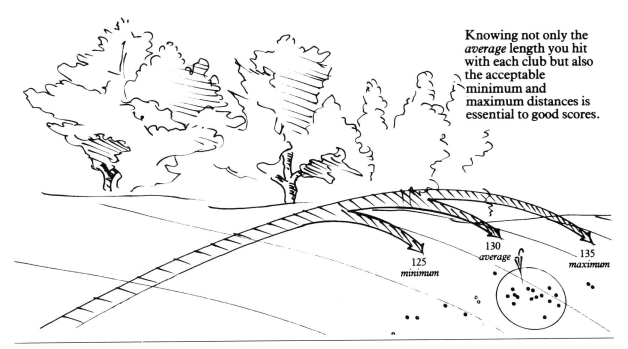

Knowing not only the *average* length you hit with each club but also the acceptable minimum and maximum distances is essential to good scores.

125
minimum

130
average

135
maximum

With this information we are establishing the target area for the played club, in this case the No. 5 iron. Now, pace off the average length and the maximum and minimum lengths. Note them in yards and paces, and keep them in mind or marked on a sample score card when you are planning your round.

Longer-hitting players will have a greater distance gap between club numbers than will short-hitters. Weaker players, senior men, ladies, and juniors do not, therefore, benefit from having more than every other number club in a set, for example, Nos. 3, 5, 7, and 9, or Nos. 4, 6, 8, and pitching wedge, in irons.

Length of shot can be spoken of in two ways:

Length of carry. The distance the ball travels from the club until it returns to earth—to its pitch point.

The shot's total length. This is the length of carry *plus* eventual distance the ball rolls.

The higher the flight trajectory the ball has, the shorter the distance it will roll. Conversely, the lower the flight the longer the roll. Ball performance must, of course, be qualified by weather and soil conditions and by local course characteristics. As your golf game develops, knowledge of how long a carry the different club lofts will give you is valuable when selecting the right club for the situation, for example, when playing to a green that has a hazard in front of it.

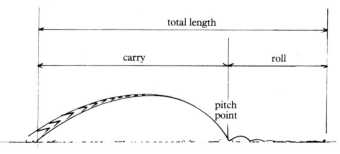

For shots over hazards, etc., knowing the "carry" distance you have for the different clubs can save some strokes per round.

Playing the course

The eighteen holes of the course contain a mixture of play areas and problem areas. The idea is now to establish *your* play areas according to *your* playing skills.

You should base your analysis of a golf hole on your knowledge of your present playing capabilities. For instance, an out-of-bounds down the right-hand side of the fairway will worry a slicer more than a player who hooks the ball, while a bunker on the left of the green is feared more by the hooker than the slicer.

When planning your trip from tee to green, try to think one shot ahead, working out from which position you can, with the least amount of trouble, play your next shot. This way of thinking is the basis for creating your road-map from tee to green. And, even after arriving there, a long putt sometimes has to be planned in the same way, to give a simple second putt. Once the road-map is clear, then you should just concentrate on one shot at a time. Each shot now has a target area from where the next shot is to be played.

But "The best laid plans of mice and men . . . ." Few rounds go exactly as planned, and that is, of course, a major part of golf's challenge and attraction. A wayward shot will result either in a new plan being quickly made in order to get back to your original route, or in the formation of a completely new plan, but both these must be based on a realistic appraisal of your capabilities.

This "safety-first" way of challenging the course can appear rather dull, but if it is a good score you want, plan a realistically attainable playing route. The excitement will come, don't you worry!

Par—the course's and yours

Each hole has a par printed on the score-card. Par is two putts plus one, two, or three long shots, depending upon whether the hole is par 3, 4, or 5. Par is only interesting when you play such special competition forms as bogey, etc. When you play a medal or stroke competition, it is the sum of the number of strokes that you take for each hole minus your handicap that counts.

When you make a round plan, you are in fact establishing your own par for the course *for that day*. Many golfers make the mistake of still playing against the scorecard's par. This is an unrealistic way of competing, and it provides for disappointing results.

For many scratch-handicap golfers, par is a barrier, and going under par is akin to going under water—you can stay there a while but sooner or later you have to come up again! This is mainly because these players do not see themselves as "better-than-par" players, despite the fact that they are capable of going under par on probably more than seventy-five per cent of the holes on the course. For these players, a round plan is the first step to changing that self-image and lowering their scores.

For the new player, of course, making par (the scorecard's!) is an interesting and necessary success; even more so is the first birdie (one stroke less than par). So par is not to be ignored, but it is your result as compared with your own planned par for the course that can provide the realistic successes.

PLAYER

MY PAR

Hole	White	Red	Par	Hcp	Score	Player		Scorer	
							2	1	2
1	400	335	4	7	5				
2	160	145	3	17	4				
3	480	410	5	11	6				
4	360	305	4	1	5				
5	350	310	4	5	5				
6	155	135	3	15	3				
7	295	265	4	9	5				
8	175	150	3	13	4				
9	380	315	4	3	5				
OUT	2755	2370	34						

SCORER _____

PLAYER _____

COMPETITION

DATE

MY PAR

Hcp 21   Score

Hole	White	Red	Par	Hcp	Score	Player		Scorer	
							2	1	2
10	360	305	4	8	5				
11	130	110	3	18	3				
12	355	310	4	2	5				
13	515	465	5	12	7				
14	200	175	3	6	3				
15	440	400	5	14	6				
16	340	290	4	4	5				
17	345	320	4	10	5				
18	455	415	5	16	6				
IN	3140	2790	37						
OUT	2755	2370	34						
Total	5895	5160	71	Gross					
SSS	72	72		Hcp					
				Net					

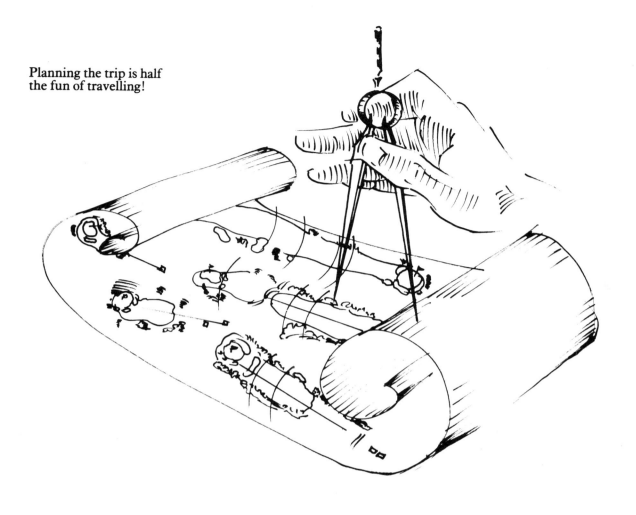

Planning the trip is half
the fun of travelling!

Knowing the course

To improve your golf, you have to learn to
know yourself, but you must also know the
course. Each course is different and, as we
mentioned earlier, is constantly changing. It
is, therefore, necessary that any course you
want to compete successfully on should be
mapped out thoroughly. The following information must be acquired in order to plan
not only from the tee but also to be able to
plan the most economical clearing-up of the
unplanned situations that will inevitably
arise.

1. The distance from tee to the near
   side of any trouble that can be
   reached with the first shot.
2. The width of the fairway where you
   expect your first shot to finish. (If
   you judge this area to be too narrow,
   then play shorter to a wider area.)
3. The length of carry necessary to hit
   over any hazards lying near to the
   finish of your first shot.

The above three points are the same for each
of the "transport" shots you require until
you come to the shot into the green. The

When choosing a target area, be sure that you would normally have a 75 per cent chance of hitting that area.

distance from the previous target area to the next *plus* the width of that area are standard measures for judging if the target is both near enough and large enough to hit with *at least a seventy-five per cent* chance of success.

When playing to the green, the length and shape of this target area should be known. The choice of club can be affected by up to three or four numbers, depending upon whether the flag is placed short or long on the green. The shape of the green is important, as many greens are narrow at some places and, for most players, a long

putt from a broader stretch of green is preferable to a shorter chip, pitch, or sand shot.

The distance from bunkers guarding the green to the center of the green is worthwhile noting. This is due to the illusion that many such bunkers give of being closer to the green than they really are.

Generally speaking, the distance of all sand and water hazards from either tee or green (whichever is closer) should be noted, so that you can calculate the distance from wherever you are on the course to any hazards that may affect shot planning. The length of the hole from respective tee to the center of the green is found on the scorecard. So a little simple arithmetic can give you a bearing on your position in relation to the green and surrounding hazards.

Summary

Getting to know your present playing capacity and establishing the plan of attack that will beat the course of the day is a stimulating challenge. It is a give-and-take experience that fosters personal characteristics that can even be useful in daily life.

Such decisions as whether to attack a hole or "seduce" it, and whether to challenge with the first shot or play safe, affect scores as much as improved swing technique.

Try, therefore, to give time to planning your golf rounds so that you can get full benefit from your technical, mental, and physical skills.

Chapter 7
THE MENTAL GAME

by Lars-Erik Sandler

Why play golf? Ask this question in a golf club and you will be met by some very strange stares! But it is a valid question now, when we are going to talk a lot about the mental side of the game. So, what motivates us to play golf?

Because it is fun, it is exciting, and challenging. In other words, golf is very good medicine for the soul. It relaxes and stimulates.

Now, most of us train our technique all the time, and we work on strategy and maybe even on our physical fitness, in order to improve our game. But how about our mental approach?

Many golfers will tell you that the game is ninety per cent psychology and ten per cent technique, and even if this is an exaggeration, it is true to say that psychology is an important part of the game. Of course, golf contains a lot more than just psychology, but mental attitude will dictate, to a surprisingly large extent, how well you will play.

In a way, we can compare golf to life. Happiness is the goal that most of us have in life, and happiness means achieving satisfaction, pleasure, and harmony. Luckily for us, and for the future of mankind, happiness is a goal that we never quite achieve, so we spend our life searching for it, moving forward continually, exploring new paths. Success is often followed by failure, in a never-ending cycle. So it is with golf.

A round of golf can be likened to your path through life. Indeed, there is the wiseacre who says that life is like a golf ball, first a lot of hard blows and then you end up in a hole . . . On the way through life, you meet with difficulties, successes, failures. But the round of golf is, in one way, better than the path through life, because a round is never like the previous one or the one to come. The next round may be better, or worse, than the previous. You can replay a round, but you cannot relive your life.

No matter how good you are, every part of your golf game can be made better, for instance, your swing technique, your putting, and even your physical fitness. But you can also improve your mental approach to the game, your "psychological fitness." This is often referred to simply as "routine." How do you acquire routine? Usually, the only way is through experience, playing round after round, practice session after practice session.

Normally, when you train technique you go out on the practice range and you hit more balls per unit of time than you do when you are playing a round. From each practice shot you hit, you learn something. You gain an experience. Each experience is deposited in your "experience bank," that is, your brain. So your brain acquires more experiences in a short time on the practice range than on the course. In the same way, you can train your "golfing mind" so that it

The golfer who has taught himself to think positively can block all thought of hazards and rough and instead see only the clear flight of the intended shot and its landing in the intended target area.

assimilates more experiences per unit of time than you would if you were out on the course, playing golf.

Positive thinking = good golf

Your mind can govern the success or failure of your actions. What happens is this. You form a picture in your mind of what is going to happen. This picture is signalled to your subconscious, and if it finds it acceptable, that is, if it considers it to be within the realms of possibility *for you*, it will have a beneficial effect on the action that ensues. The trouble is that the subconscious stores, as if in a computer memory, all experience, both negative and positive. Suppose that you say to yourself, "I'm not going to play the ball into that rough," you are sending a negative signal to the brain, which it will accept if you do not send some *positive* signals about what is going to happen or what you would like to happen. If the negative signals are not blocked or "over-powered" by positive signals, the result will most often be that you hit the ball right into that rough. So lesson 1 is *Think positively*. The mental training that we are going to describe now is going to teach you to think positively, to steer your thoughts into positive channels, and to send to the sub-conscious positive pictures of what you want to happen. You are going to build up a positive attitude about what will happen to the ball when you hit it. Winners see what they want to happen, losers fear what might happen.

The mental game of golf is all about being an optimistic realist. You must be able to judge what you actually can and cannot do. If you are truly aware of your own capabilities, you can, by only asking the possible of yourself, create a positive picture that

Target and ball-flight practice. Build up confidence in your ability to hit the ball into a given area with a given club. Program your subconscious to accept this.

your subconscious will be able to accept completely. Of course, you are still not going to succeed with every shot, but your success rate will be higher. To begin with, you must have a reasonably stable golfing technique so that your subconscious is going to get a regular positive feedback about your game. As a beginner, you succeeded with, say, five out of ten shots. As a low handicapper, you would succeed with, say, eight out of ten shots. Your successful shots are not necessarily perfect, but the result and the expected result (the picture of what you wanted to do) will often be one and the same thing.

Practice thinking about target and ball flight. To begin with, stand on the driving range. Pick out different targets and use different clubs to hit the ball to them. Think about ball flight, direction, the area in which the ball will land and how it will roll. Don't hit more than five balls to begin with. Take a rest and do it again. The object of this is to make you think automatically: "If I want to hit the ball to that target with this club, the direction must be this, the flight of the ball should be the following, the area of landing will be there, and the ball will roll such and such a length." When you have done this many times, and it is beginning to work for you, you begin to build up confidence in your ability to achieve what you set out to

do, or in other words, what you have told your subconscious you are going to do. To put it another way, you are programming your subconscious to accept that you have a certain level of skill. When you feel that you have trained your subconscious sufficiently, continue your mental training on the golf course. Play just a couple of holes to begin with. The next time you play, increase the number until in the end you can play a whole round, thinking positively and achieving success automatically.

If, on the other hand, you cheat yourself into believing that you are a better golfer than you actually are, you will be dismayed to find that you have not managed to cheat your subconscious. It *knows*. So many past experiences of what you can and cannot do have programmed your subconscious so that it will not believe you if you say that you can pitch your way over that bunker, short stopping at the flag. Your conscious plans or statements must be acceptable to your subconscious, because it is your subconscious that influences what actually happens. *Therefore, much of your golfing success is going to depend on how much you can remove the psychological barriers that you have built into your subconscious about your golfing ability.* "I'm never going to hit the ball that far; I'll never get it over that bunker; I'm sure I'll put it into that water hazard." That is negative thinking and will produce negative results.

So what can you do about negative thinking? First and foremost, assess the situation realistically. Is your golf swing technically good enough for that shot? Are you physically strong enough to achieve that length? If you can answer "yes" to these questions, you have the prerequisites necessary to make it. If you know from experience that your swing is not good enough or that you are simply not strong enough to hit the ball that hard, then choose a target that is realistic. Both your conscious and your subconscious will be able to agree about that. If you liken the mind to an iceberg, the conscious will be the part above the water, while the subconscious is the part underneath. And it is the submerged part of the iceberg, driven by the ocean currents, that decides where the iceberg is going to float. So what you want to do is to influence the submerged part of your mind, your subconscious. And what is it that influences your subconscious? It is, as indicated earlier, the accumulation of experience. If the experiences accumulated every time you hit a golf ball are good, then you are going to have a positive attitude to each shot that you are about to take. If bad, then you are going to go into each shot situation already beaten.

Good golfers get better by continual training; they practice in different types of situations, ball lies, and so on. Each time they hit a ball, they accumulate the experience in their subconscious, thus building up a data base about their own ability, what is possible and what is not. Now most weekend golfers do not have the time to invest in this kind of training, so the method we suggest here is a good alternative, as it combines the above method with a method that crams a lot of "experience" into a short length of time, without having to be out on the golf course.

To put it simply, what you do is that you imagine yourself in various golfing situations, you consider for yourself how best to play them, and then still in your imagination, you play them, hitting the ball as you had planned, thus giving your subconscious a direct positive experience to add to the positive data base. You see, the brain has difficulty in separating what has happened in reality and what has happened in the imagination. *So repeated exercises in the imagination, which end up positively, will*

accumulate a large, positive data base in your subconscious. If you do it regularly, all the negative attitudes you have had about your golfing ability will be swamped by the new and positive experiences you have been imagining in your mind's eye. You can carry out these mental training sessions at irregular intervals, or you can decide to train systematically in this way, for instance by deciding that you are going to have a mental training session before you leave for work in the morning or as soon as you get home in the evening. An example of the kind of golfing problem that you can remedy with this type of mental training is the slice when you are confronted with a hazard of some kind, say, water. Normally, you do not slice your shots, but just on the hole where there is a water hazard to the right, you have a tendency to slice. Apart from avoiding a slice, you need a little extra length at this hole in order to get into a good position for the next shot. But you have a mental block about this: as soon as you try to get in that extra length, always with the danger spot on the right in mind, you hit a slice. Plan to get rid of this mental block by working at it during, say, a month. Check on your progress by using the development charts described in the previous chapter.

Apart from playing and training as often as you can, you also go in for mental training, so that your subconscious receives a steady number of positive messages about this golfing situation that you find so difficult. We divide your mental training into two stages, the first being the introduction to the second. Plan to have such a session every second day during the month.

Mental Training Session Part 1
Find a room in which you will not be disturbed. Your bedroom is probably the best place. Put on your favorite piece of soothing, relaxing music—not loud. Relax as much as you can. Breathe deeply and go over your body, bit by bit. Feel how your calm breathing is relaxing you more and more. Start at your toes and "make" them

In your mind, you are confident at the tee;

your shot has good ball-flight;

landing well in the target area;

you are satisfied with your result.

feel relaxed by tensing them and then relaxing them. Now work your way up along your body, calf, knee, thigh, and so on. Tense and relax, tense and relax, until you can feel the difference between the muscles that are being tensed and those that are relaxed. Your whole being will go into a state of deep relaxation and you can let your mind wander in quiet thoughts. After about fifteen minutes, "wake" yourself by moving your toes, fingers, and hands slightly. Now take some deep breaths, stretch and bend your arms a few times, and then open your eyes. Why do you need to do this? Firstly, your body and mind will feel all the better for a little relaxation. Your whole system begins to work at a lower rate, and the result is that you begin to rest. Secondly, by training your muscles to relax completely, you are increasing your ability to achieve a state of total mental relaxation, which is important in our mental training, for the following reason.

When your mind is relaxed, it is far easier for your subconscious to receive and assimilate signals. In other words, you can influence your subconscious more easily when you are in a state of relaxation.

Some people can achieve a state of deep relaxation more easily than others. Those who have difficulty in relaxing may need to work at it for two, three, or even four weeks. If you are lucky, you can learn this almost at your first training session.

Mental Training Session Part 2
Part 1 puts you into a state of deep relaxation. Once you are there, breathing deeply and calmly, you lead your mind into your problem situation.

Imagine that you are standing at the tee addressing the ball, and the water hazard is off to your right. Go all the way through the sequence of action that is going to put the ball exactly in the target area: the swing, impact, ball flight, direction, landing area, and roll. When you have done this, that is, fulfilled your intentions with a positive result, let your thoughts wander for a minute or so without thinking about anything special. Now "wake" yourself up as in Part 1.

The positive message that you have now sent to your subconscious will, when repeated, accumulate until the positive outweighs the negative, and the psychological "block" in your subconscious is removed.

Golf *should* be challenging!

Most of us are attracted by the thought of doing something that is challenging. By rising to the challenge, we use resources within ourselves that, often, we did not know existed, and in this way we develop as people. That is how children develop, too. They dare to do things that are new and strange: the first time they stand upright without holding on to something is a moment of great triumph for them, and rightly so. Challenge and excitement are the spices of life. If we protect ourselves from these, we will find life limited, boring, and without interest.

In situations of excitement, the body adapts to meet the situation. The heart beats more quickly, your attention is sharpened, and all your senses are alive and working at top speed. Excitement gives you a charge, which you often experience as both exhilarating and frightening. Your mind will find it "painfully nice." Sometimes, this experience is felt as only painful. The excitement makes you feel ill. If this happens regularly in such situations, you are going to build up a bank of negative attitudes to these exciting situations.

The opposite extreme to this state of high excitement is a complete lack of excitement. Some people have managed to protect themselves from all that is exciting and challenging in life, and this can even be transferred to the golf course. The game seems boring, nothing happens.

Naturally, neither of these extremes is to be recommended. The remedy for the high-excitement extreme is, of course, to lower the level. Practice on the course on a day when there are few people around to give you stress. Reconstruct a situation that, last time you played, had you over-excited. Begin by simplifying it, so that you get out of the situation easily. Then make it more and more difficult, until finally it is super-difficult.

Plan to carry out this kind of training in the long term. Before you leave home, go through what you intend to practice. Then go and carry out your plan. When you get home again, evaluate what happened. Plan your next session according to the results you got from this session. Each positive experience that you gained will add to your data base of positive thought about your golf game.

The other extreme, in which you find the game boring and uninspiring, is much more easy to deal with. Normally, if you find something uninspiring, you stop doing it, unless you are forced to. But you don't want to give up golf, you just want to get out of a fit of boredom with the game. So change your way of playing. Play with new people, who can bring back the excitement to the game. Or play much more offensively, exposing yourself thereby to situations that are going to be challenging and make demands on your skill and nerve. Start working long-term with the professional at your club, with a definite aim in mind, for instance, to get greater length out of your shots. Establish a goal with him and work at achieving it.

If all of these methods do not work, then your general apathy about the game might be because you are playing too much. Take a break for a week or two. Go watch football or do something else with your free time. You have to enjoy playing and to be "hungry" for it in order to play well. After a couple of weeks' abstinence, you are going to want to get at it like a tiger at a lamb.

Thou shalt not steal!

As a child, you have probably skipped school at least once, especially if there was going to be a particularly tough test that day. You wandered around town enjoying the freedom—but wasn't there a gnawing feeling in the pit of your stomach? Bad conscience, fear of punishment, call it what you like. Have you felt that feeling now that you're grown up? I have! And you've guessed right, it was when I was on the golf course, while my family was waiting somewhere for me, or a colleague at work was standing in for me when I should have been there. I was stealing my golfing time from something else. People were getting left in the lurch, and it was my fault.

Addiction to golf is a serious psychological problem, just like gambling. You can get hooked on it. If you do, the symptoms can grow from psychological to physical. You begin to feel bad—you get stress symptoms, ulcers, and high blood pressure. This is dangerous for all concerned, and the only way to avoid it is to give every part of your life its own time—family, work, leisure time, and golf. OK, I know, many people will say that golf *is* leisure time, but we golfers know otherwise, so let's agree that your life has those four parts, each as important as the others. If you plan your time properly, with agreed time for everything, then you will have no cause to feel guilty about being on the golf course. Your family will know that every Saturday morning, for

instance, you are playing a full round, and your colleagues at work will know that you finish early on Tuesday to play nine holes. And everybody will accept that, *if* they know that you are not going to be sneaking off to the course whenever the bug bites you. So remember, don't steal your golf from anything or anyone. Then nobody will begrudge you the time you spend out on the course.

Are you a worried golfer?

The human body is a fantastic piece of equipment which has an automatic "defence" system that keeps the various parts of the organism in working order. If body temperature rises above normal, the automatic cooling system starts, and you begin to sweat. Likewise, if anything else starts to function abnormally, the defence system sets off an antidote to counteract that and to restore the balance to normal.

If, however, you expose yourself to strain time after time, and now we are talking about both physical and mental strain, the human organism's ability to counteract this and to restore normality to the system is reduced.

Take a beginner at golf. He is out on his first or second round ever, and there is a foursome behind him, waiting to start and, as golfers do, watching. In such circumstances, his fellow players should not make the beginner drive off first. Such a nervous strain might turn anyone off the game for good. Golf is there to be enjoyed, not to turn you into a nervous wreck!

What happens to the beginner in such a situation or to the able golfer in deep trouble in the rough? Well, this may sound far-fetched, but the answer is that they react exactly like their prehistoric forefathers reacted when they found themselves in, for them, comparable situations—when for instance they were threatened by wild animals or some other form of danger. The body starts to produce adrenalin and noradrenalin, popularly called "stress hormones," to prime itself to cope with the situation. An increase in the production of stress hormones will increase blood pressure and make your heart beat faster and harder. This allows the blood to flow quickly to the muscles, increasing their ability to react quickly and strongly.

The problem with this reaction is that it was created for survival in a world in which we no longer live. Our prehistoric forefathers had to increase their concentration, speed of reaction, and strength in order to survive violent physical action. Their sharp increase of stress-hormone production was followed by a violent reaction (battle or flight) which released all that pent-up energy. Today, we have that release all too seldom. A stress-filled situation increases our stress hormones, but when no violent release occurs, we end up bottling the stress

129

inside and getting headaches, ulcers, and so on. Too much stress is not good and the body will not be able to react properly to cope with the situation. But neither is too little stress good, because this does not produce enough sharpened concentration and strength to enable the body to react sufficiently. Illustrated is a graph that shows how performance varies according to the amount of stress experienced.

If you find that your golf game exposes you to too much mental strain, you will develop a negative attitude to the game and your golf will suffer. *If you can set your sights at a level that is within your capabilities, your subconscious will be building up a store of positive thoughts about your game, and you will be able to have a positive attitude.* So even if a shot does not turn out right, you know that the next can be a winner. Improvement is always around the corner.

How to change concentration gear

Despite all that we have said above about stress-filled golfing situations, one of the very best things about playing golf is that it enables you to relax from the cares of everyday life. This enables you to concentrate your mind on the game at hand. Good golf requires mental energy and involvement, and these will be released automatically if you are relaxed, ready to enjoy the game, and motivated to play well.

But you should not try to keep your level of energy and concentration at top pitch throughout the game. This would drain you of all physical and mental energy within a very short time, and your game will deteriorate as the game goes along. The thing to do is to "charge" your mental and physical

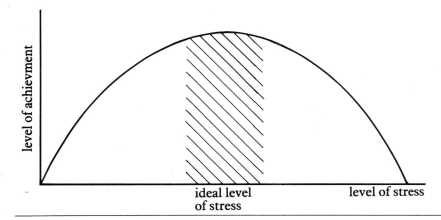

In a tense golfing situation, or in any other situation that requires an effort, if we feel too little stress we will fail to produce the necessary effort, while too much stress will produce too many stress hormones, and this will result in a tensed, cramped body that will not be able to swing the club properly.

"batteries" at the beginning of the game and then *not* to drain them of your "electricity" each time you address and hit the ball. Use only what is necessary in the required situation. Then "recharge" your batteries in between strokes by relaxing physically as well as mentally.

Charge your batteries before the game by looking forward to it with anticipation—this is going to be fun! Increase your anticipation by building up a good "relationship" with your clubs and other equipment. Check your clubs, finger them lovingly, they are going to be part and parcel of the enjoyable game in front of you. Pick out your favorite golf balls and take them one by one in your hand. Feel their shape. Close your eyes and imagine how the ball will behave exactly as you want it to. See in your mind's eye its beautiful path through the air and hear the murmurs of acclamation from your fellow players. Build up a positive picture of what is going to happen. Then get your other gear together—ball markers, green repairer, pen, tees, and so on. Now relax for a while and chat with friends or do whatever you want to do to put yourself in a good humor. "Play" a little on the practice range or green, so that you are in a good mood when you get to the first tee.

When you drive off, use your full concentration. As soon as you have hit the ball, *relax*. Think about something else. Admire the natural surroundings. Talk with your fellow players (but without disturbing the one who is playing). As your turn comes for the next shot, you begin a slow build-up of concentration again. The legendary Walter Hagen used to say, "Don't forget to sniff the flowers along the way."

We can compare this to a traffic light. When you are relaxed, with some time to go before your next shot, the light is red = stop, hold, relax. As your turn gets closer, the light turns orange, and you begin preparing yourself. Then, when you step up to the ball, you have green, and then it is *go*. All physical and nervous concentration is involved in the stroke. After the release of

Some time to go before it is your turn. Relax and enjoy the scenery.

Begin to prepare yourself for your turn.

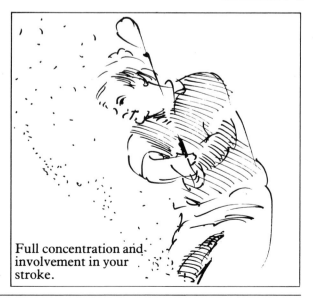

Full concentration and involvement in your stroke.

energy, the light changes, and you relax again, recharging your batteries.

The simple rules of mental golf

1. A positive attitude will produce positive results.
2. Know yourself and your capabilities.
3. Play offensively and to the full extent of your capabilities.
4. Extend yourself to meet the challenge.
5. Relax and enjoy, enjoy, enjoy!

Chapter 8
THE PHYSICAL GAME

by Rolf Wirhed

What physical qualities do you need in order to become a good golfer? The answer depends on a number of things, among them your age, how good you want to become, and what other qualities you have already. But there is one quality that good golfers must have and which you should aim at improving in yourself, and that is great flexibility in the shoulders and trunk. The good golfer has a very flexible spine, and this is most noticeable when he has reached the top of his backswing. And the top-class golfer can usually demonstrate the extreme flexibility of his shoulders by clasping his hands together straight behind his back. The elasticity means that he can start a backswing smoothly and steadily, and can reach the ideal top position without being hampered by stiffness or too much compensatory movement in the limbs.

It goes without saying that a good golfer needs to be fit and strong. Exaggerated strength is not necessary, but the important muscles, those of the back, stomach, and lower arm, should be well trained. If you want to hit the ball far, then you must have strong leg muscles (always assuming that your swing is more or less correct).

Flexibility

Let's look first at how you can check how good or bad your flexibility is. Then we will describe a number of exercises to help you develop it.

A well-trained golfer has great flexibility in the upper body, enabling him to reach the ideal top position in his backswing with smoothness and without too much compensatory movements from the limbs.

Test 1

With your back to a wall, see how far from it you can stand and still touch it with the fingertips of both hands, with your arms straight. Your arms should be at shoulder height and you should stand well-balanced on straight legs. Don't bend your knees and lean back. Measure the distance between your heels and the wall.

Test 2

Sit on a stool placed against the edge of an open door. Try to keep both your neck and lower back against the edge of the door. Lift your arms up and back over your head. Place your palms flat, one on each side of the door, and try to reach as far back as possible. Measure from the edge of the door to your fingertips.

Test 3

Try to make the fingertips of both hands touch behind your back, as in the picture. Measure the gap between your "best" and your "worst" side. Combine the results. If your fingers do not touch at all on one side, subtract the shortfall from the result.

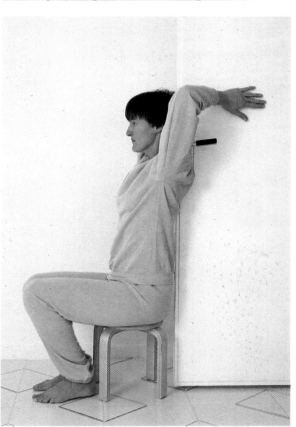

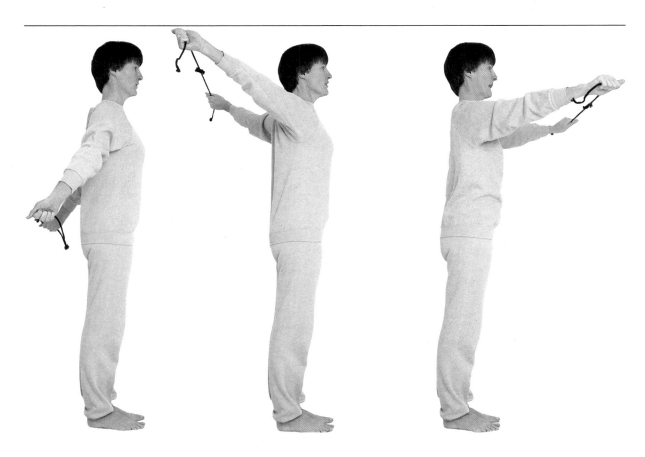

Test 4
Hold your arms straight
and see what is the
shortest piece of cord
you can stretch between
your hands while still
being able to pass your
hands over your head
and down your back.
Measure the length of
the cord.

The results of these tests will show you how flexible your shoulders really are. A top player would have a result of, say, 0. The present writer plays a lot of golf but has fairly stiff shoulders, because he was a gymnast when young and went in for too much strength training of his shoulder muscles, so his results should be taken as a warning. Now test yourself in the same way as illustrated and compare yourself with the other results on the table. Draw your own conclusions about your flexibility!

Test No.	Top player	Author	Yourself
1	19 ins	10 ins	
2	14 ins	7¾ ins	
3	+4¾, +1½ ins	−7¾, −4 ins	
4	39¼ ins	55 ins	

To establish a "flexibility figure", you can subtract result Nos. 1, 2, and 3 from result No. 4. This means that the top player has a flexibility figure of
$39¼ − 4¾ − 1½ − 14 − 19 = 0$.
The author has
$55 + 7¾ + 4 − 7¾ − 10 = 49$.

With arms raised out from your sides to shoulder height, pass as far as you can through a normal doorway. Your arms will be pushed behind in the position that you adopted when you were measuring flexibility. The muscles affected by the exercise are primarily the large pectorals and the front part of the deltoids. If you are going to use the stretching method, then try to relax the pectoral muscles as much as possible, and carefully push forward an inch or two until you feel resistance in the front of your shoulders. Hold this position for about thirty seconds, then shake yourself loose and repeat the procedure three or four times.

If you are going to use the contraction-relaxation-stretching method, then adopt the same position, but start by pressing with your hands as hard as you can against the wall for six seconds, then relax two seconds in the same position. Now lean carefully forward an inch or two until you feel the muscles in the front of your shoulders resisting. Stay in that position for about ten seconds. Repeat the procedure another three or four times.

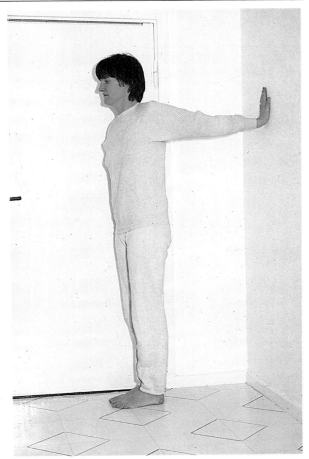

(*Right*) Another exercise for the pectorals. Palm against the wall and push forward with the shoulder.

The exercises shown on this and the following pages will increase the flexibility of your shoulders and trunk or keep you as flexible as you are already.

Do the exercises a few times every week. Keeping flexible is a must for older golfers; it not only helps them to maintain their swing but it also prevents muscle injury, especially in the back and shoulders. The exercises shown are well-known stretching exercises, in which you extend, or stretch, a muscle or a group of muscles for about thirty seconds at a time. Then you relax the muscle slowly. *Never* stretch or relax quickly. Do the exercises slowly and remember that they should never be painful, always pleasant.

Another, and more effective, method is a development of the above. You adopt the same position as for stretching but, before you begin stretching, you contract the muscle hard for six seconds. (It has been shown that, if a muscle is contracted hard, it is easier to relax it immediately afterwards.) Then you relax the muscle for two seconds,

and finally you stretch it for ten seconds. Repeat this exercise—six seconds' contraction, two seconds' relaxation, ten seconds' stretching—between three and five times. This method is known as the *contraction-relaxation-stretching* method. Illustrated are exercises that will increase the flexibility of the muscles in your shoulders, thus making it easier for you to improve the smoothness of your swing.

Regular training with these exercises will soon bring a measurable improvement. Take test measurements first, as on the previous page, then train regularly for four weeks and check again. When you feel that you are sufficiently flexible, one training period per week will be enough to maintain this condition. Older people will find it more difficult to improve their flexibility, but if they stick at these exercises, they can achieve amazingly good results. Among the positive effects of this kind of exercise is that the reduction in mobility that naturally sets in with increasing old age can be checked.

You do not need to have expensive training equipment to increase the strength and flexibility of your shoulder muscles. A hand towel will do very well for the exercises illustrated here.

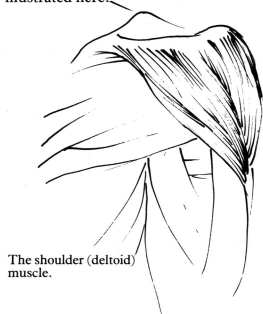

The shoulder (deltoid) muscle.

The large pectoral muscle. These two muscles are heavily involved in the golf swing.

"Dry" your back, pulling the higher arm down with the lower. Then pull the lower arm up an extra bit with the higher one. Do this ten times with the left arm uppermost, then ten

Hold the towel taut as shown and "dry" the back of your neck. Make sure you grip the towel so that you can pull one arm with the other,

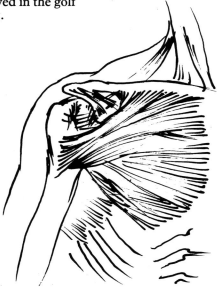

times with the right arm uppermost.

Hold the towel with arms straight and hands just far enough apart to place it alternately in front of and behind your trunk. Do this twenty times with the left hand uppermost and twenty times with the right hand uppermost.

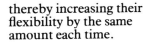

thereby increasing their flexibility by the same amount each time.

Hold the towel with your hands just far enough apart for you to raise your hands above your head. Your arms should be straight and the towel taut. Move your arms forward and backward twenty to thirty times.

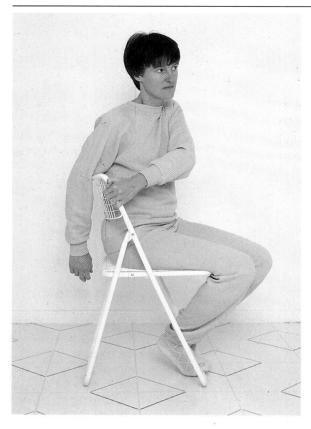

Sit on a chair and draw
alternately with your left
and right hand in the
back of the chair, as
shown.

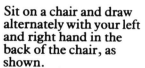
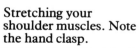

Stretching your
shoulder muscles. Note
the hand clasp.

Lower-arm stretching.
Push the palm of your
hand against the wall
while you push your
elbow down toward the
ground.

Strength training

The good golfer combines flexibility with adequate strength. Strength training tends to make the muscles stiff and short, a fact that has led to such training being considered unnecessary or even undesirable for golfers. This is wrong. Bearing in mind what we now know about the connection between flexibility and strength, the best advice—especially to young golfers who want to try for the top—must be this. Build up your general strength (throughout your body) by means of suitable exercises. Later, concentrate on specific strength training for your legs, back, stomach, and lower arms. At the same time, you should train especially with flexibility exercises for the back and shoulders.

The hormonally determined difference in strength between men and women is indicated by how much farther men can drive a golf ball. In matters of swing technique, however, a good female player is equal to a good male player. And the difference between male and female strength is less in the leg muscles than in the lower arms. So it is sound advice for women who want to improve their game to do strength training for the back and lower arms. Considerable improvement in performance can be achieved by this.

When strength-training a muscle, you should always be aware of the following principles.

1. The endurance of a muscle is developed by tiring it with "low-load" movements repeated many times.
Training a muscle in this way will increase the number of small blood vessels (capillaries) in the muscle. It then becomes easier for the heart to supply the working muscle with oxygen and nourishment. This means that the muscle can execute the same movement a greater number of times before it tires. In other words, its endurance increases.

Endurance training may consist, for example, of loading the muscle to fifty per cent of its maximum capacity. In this strength-training exercise, a suitable weight would be 45 lb, or the maximum of what you can lift with one hand. If we say that you could, before starting training, lift 20 lb twenty-five times and 45 lb just once, you will find that after exercising regularly with a low load, you should be able to lift the 20-lb weight perhaps forty to fifty times, while your maximum strength increases very little, and you can manage no more than a generous 45 lb.

2. Maximum strength is increased by training with weights just below your maximum capacity.
If your maximum is 45 lb, then you should train with weights that are eighty to ninety per cent of this. Regular training will progressively increase your maximum strength, and you will be able to lift 50 lb, 55 lb, and so on. As you improve your maximum strength, you increase the weights, so that you are always training at about eighty to ninety per cent of your full potential.

Carry out your weight training systematically. Do six repeat lifts (repetitions, or "reps"), then rest two minutes. These six reps are known as a "set." Continue with another set (six reps) and rest two minutes again. The normal "dose" when training your maximum strength is three sets of six reps each, in other words a total of eighteen reps with a weight which is eighty per cent of your maximum capacity. This will also improve your endurance somewhat, but not so quickly as when you train according to method 1, above.

Table showing the weights, reps, and sets you use to develop different types of strength.

	Endurance	Speed	Max. strength
% of max. potential	25 – 50	50 – 80	80 – 100
No. of reps	more than 40	c. 10	1 – 6
No. of sets	5	4	3

Back muscle exercises

One leg at a time off the floor.

Hands, shoulders, and chest off the floor.

Right arm and left leg off the floor. Then left arm and right leg.

Stomach muscle exercises

Arms crossed on chest. Raise shoulders as much as possible off the floor.

Lie on your back and raise your behind off the floor.

Walk around on your toes and hands only. Stay fully stretched.

Note: the above three are given in increasing degrees of difficulty. Don't overdo it in the beginning.

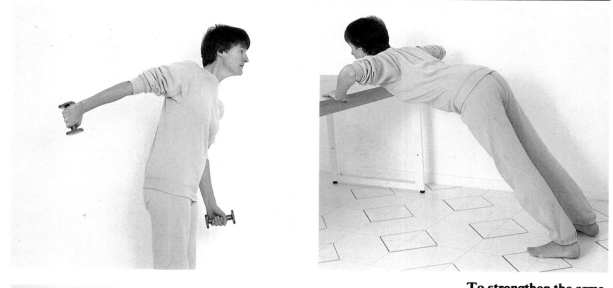

To strengthen the arms

(Above left) Begin with light dumb-bells and graduate to heavier. Lift the dumb-bell back with a straight arm. Alternate arms.

(Above) The easiest push-up is from a table or chair.

(Left) Push-ups from a kneeling position are somewhat harder to do.

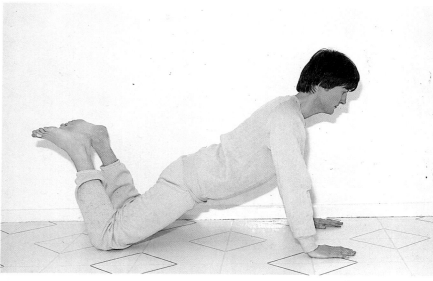

(Left) The "full" push-up.

"Pull-ups" are a good way to strengthen arm muscles.

(*Above*) Lie on your back under a table and pull yourself up, keeping your back straight.

(*Right*) If you have access to them, use rings for pull-ups, otherwise anything else suitable will do.

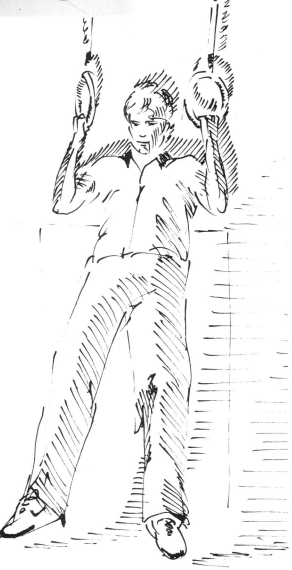

Golfers who are aiming at a marked improvement in their game should work on the program indicated in the column for endurance training, that is, many reps with low loads. Follow this program three times per week during the off-season and at least once a week in the playing season.

N.B. Only after a winter of endurance training should you go on to speed training! The exercises for speed training should be done as regularly as those for endurance training.

Strength training is often equated with lifting weights and using dumbbells, but to develop good all-round strength, there is an advantage in using your own body as the "weights". This is especially true when developing the kind of strength needed for playing golf. Illustrated are variations on exercises for strengthening the stomach, back, and arms. The stomach and back exercises should concentrate primarily on developing endurance (that is, lots of reps). The arm exercises should be chosen according to whether you want to build up endurance, speed, or maximum strength.

(*Left*) While holding dumb-bells, raise your arms out from your sides as high as you can.

(*Right*) Kneel between two chairs and slowly raise yourself with your hands on the seats of the chairs.

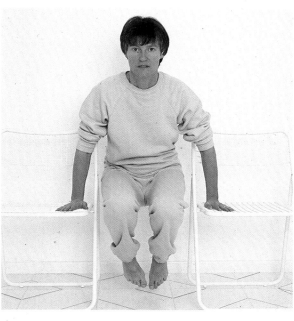

(*Left*) Go down on your hands and feet, as in the picture, and simply raise your hands, one at the time, from the floor.

Static exercising. With your back against the wall, slide down into a sitting position until your thighs are parallel to the ground. Keep this position as long as you can.

Running

The best way for a golfer to strengthen his or her leg muscles is running, which has the added benefit of providing necessary fitness training at the same time. For top-level golfers, three 3-mile runs per week out of season and one, preferably two, runs in the playing season should be included in their training. The resulting improvement in condition allows them to keep their concentration at a high level throughout a competition. The intensive practice required of today's best golfers also demands a great fitness. You will get nowhere today without hard practice with club and ball. In recent years, skills have increased among the elite players and competition has stiffened considerably.

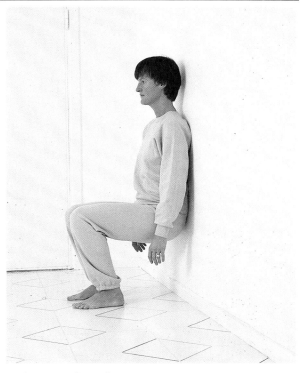

One-legged jumps until you get tired. Then on the other leg.

Take a number of extra long strides, bending as much as you can with the foremost knee.

More leg exercises

Rise up on your toes, one foot at a time. If necessary, support yourself with one hand on a wall or a tree.

Even the weekend golfer can benefit from good condition. If you run to improve your general fitness and to strengthen your leg muscles, you should intersperse it with strength exercises.

Going for runs on the golf course is an obvious way for golfers to organize their training. The surface is kind on the feet and the membrane covering of the bones, while the length of the holes will enable you to keep a check on how far you have run. You soon learn where and when you can run without disturbing games in progress. An 18-hole run that bypasses sensitive areas makes about 3 miles. If you break off at every third hole and carry out some leg-strengthening exercises, you have a perfect pattern for your general training.

Your willingness to train, your enjoyment of matches, and your ability to press on when things go wrong during a competition

Sideways hops on one leg.

Jump up in the air, pulling both knees as close to the chest as you

can (but more than in the picture).

will increase in proportion to your improvement in fitness and strength. This is true for almost all sports. Marksmen, for example, need to be very fit, and it would be strange if golfers did not benefit from being so.

General fitness, and also leg strength, are important if you are to manage to get around an 18-hole course without showing signs of fatigue. When you swing a golf club, all the movements of the arms and club take place mainly in a vertical plane. The steeper the swing, the more this is so. All the forces required to accelerate the shoulders and the club affect the legs, too. If you stood with each foot on bathroom weighing scales, it would be possible to measure the forces the leg muscles are subjected to when you drive a golf ball. Such measurements would show that, when the work load is greatest (at impact), the left leg is subjected to 1.14 times the golfer's body weight, and the right leg 0.33 times. Now if you cannot counteract these forces with an exactly equal force, you will have to compensate by bending or stretching a little in the knee and hip, which means that you will not hit cleanly. At worst, you will top or duff. So leg strength *is* important!

The lower arm and wrist

The lower arm and wrist are, of course, the most important "tool" you use to get the right speed and precision at impact. When you move your whole hand, or when you grip something, you use different types of muscles: (*a*) muscles that bend only the fingers, (*b*) muscles that bend both the wrist and the fingers, (*c*) muscles that steer the movements of the wrist, and (*d*) muscles that rotate the lower arm so that the palm of your hand points toward or away from you. Strange as it might seem, strength in these muscles is very important if you are going to be good at golf. Many weekend golfers would soon begin to play better if they trained the muscles of their lower arms and wrists regularly. This would be most marked in the case of women golfers. The

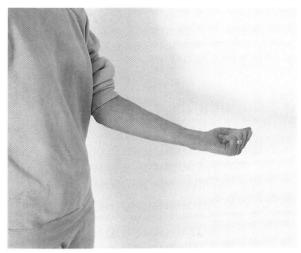

The one-handed applause uses the muscles that bend both wrists and fingers.

Women players especially should work at strengthening these muscles.

first thing that would improve would certainly be their short game and the ability to get out of difficult lies.

Test the endurance of these muscles by quickly striking your fingers against the palm of the same hand (one-handed clapping). I suspect that you will get really tired after thirty or forty claps. The muscles that you now feel are of type (*b*).

Now press your elbows to your sides. Spread your fingers wide and twist your wrists quickly so that your palms are alternately turned up and down. You will soon feel muscles of type (*d*) beginning to tire.

The illustrated exercises are for strengthening the lower arms. Use one golf club at first, gradually progressing to two taped together, as shown. The lower down the shaft you hold it, or them, the easier the exercise. If you hold it at the top of the grip, you make it much harder, of course. In the beginning, hold the club so that you are moderately tired after twenty-five reps. Do twenty-five reps with each hand. When you have done all three exercises, you will have done seventy-five reps with each hand.

Press your elbow against
your side and twist the
club as shown.

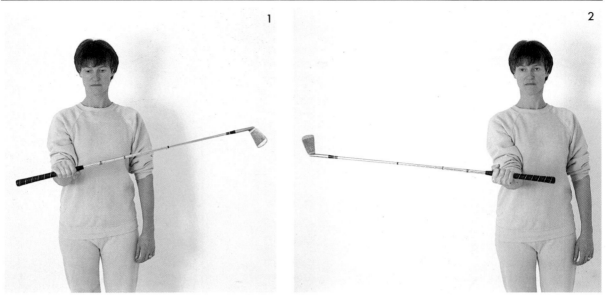

1

2

Change then to two further exercises, in which you hold the club with your normal grip. When you have become stronger, use two clubs or hold one club with just one hand at a time.

N.B. If you are thinking of trying these

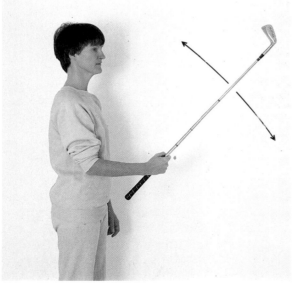

Hold your arm slightly
bent against your side so
that only your wrist is
mobile. Move the club
as shown.

Hold your arms straight
and somewhat behind
your back, while
carrying out the
illustrated exercise.

Press your elbow against your side and "write" the numbers 1 – 25 in the air, using big movements of the wrist and lower arm.

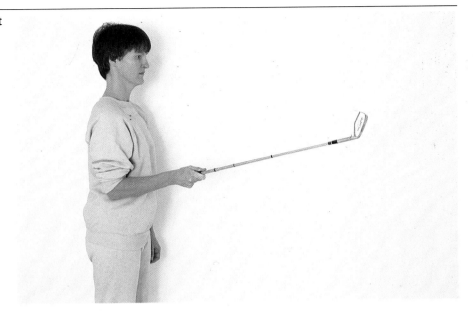

Again, "write" 1 – 25 in the air but, this time, keep your arms straight, so that all the movement comes from the shoulders and wrist.

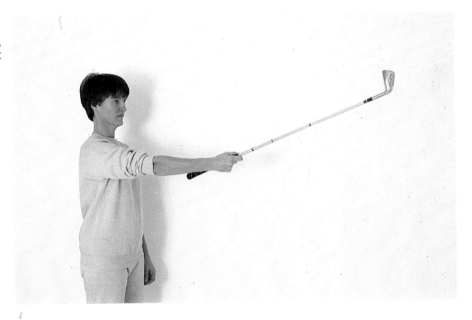

exercises, don't do them too often, for instance, three times a week. In the early weeks, do one set of each exercise, using one club only. Watch out for feelings of soreness in your elbows or the tendons in the wrists. You don't want to damage a muscle. After a few weeks of getting used to these exercises, you can begin to repeat each set of exercises once or twice. Grip the club a little way down the shaft to begin with. Increase the number of reps progressively.

Your muscles and your golf swing

There is a certain relationship between strength, flexibility, length of backswing, speed of swing, and accuracy of shot. If your goal is maximum accuracy, your backswing should be short. In fact, it should be as short as possible without your having to apply too much force at the moment of turn. If you want maximum length, the backswing should be long, but this usually produces dismal results from the point of view of accuracy. Our potential for swinging a golf club is governed by certain anatomical and physiological facts, the most important of which are described here.

Golfer A has an arm muscle that is attached closer to the center of the shoulder joint than is golfer B's arm muscle. Consequently, if both contract their muscle an equal distance, A's arm will move through a greater angle than will B's. A is thus quicker than B, with all that this entails for speed with which his clubhead hits the ball.

However, when an action requiring strength has to be carried out, B has the advantage, because his less centrally attached muscle exerts greater leverage. B is thus stronger than A. Such innate differences just have to be accepted. A has, in other words, better prospects of hitting the ball a long way.

When a muscle contracts, it can do this with varying amounts of force. A small amount gives a slow start to the movement. The shorter the distance the muscle has to contract, the slower the final speed of the movement. The same muscle can vary in strength in different situations. A fully stretched muscle can always contract with greater force than one that is only partly stretched. Research has shown that a muscle is at its strongest when it is stretched twenty per cent above its length at rest. It cannot contract at all if it is stretched under fifty per cent of its length at rest. So if you stop your

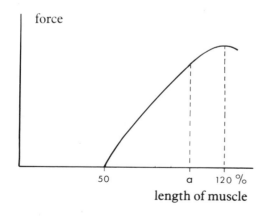

The diagram shows the connection between the power a muscle can produce in a certain situation and the length that the muscle has at the time. The muscle cannot contract at all if it is stretched under 50% of its length at rest (a). If it is stretched 20% more than its length at rest, it can contract with the greatest force (that is, it can produce the most power).

backswing too early, you are not reaching the position in which your muscles are at their strongest, and you also have a shorter distance in which to accelerate the clubhead on its way.

Another characteristic of a muscle is that it can develop more power if it is stretched and then, because the stretching movement has to be stopped abruptly, checked sharply. For example, in the backswing the muscles are stretched until the club is in the top position. If the "turn" (the transition from backswing to downswing) is abrupt, more power can be developed.

Now, if you are flexible in hips, trunk, and shoulders, it is easier to take up the optimum position (in which your muscles are stretched twenty per cent more than their length at rest) at the top of your backswing. And, if you are also strong, you can execute a gentle, smooth backswing and turn, because you do not need the extra power that would come from checking the backswing sharply at the top. A slower

check at the top gives greater precision at the turn, thus allowing you to remain in the correct swing plane during the downswing.

If, because of poor flexibility or some obstacle on the course, you are forced to make a backswing that will not allow your muscles to reach their optimum stretch and in which the distance to the ball will be too short, you must rely on the quick check at the top of the swing to give you the increased power necessary. The quicker the backswing the tauter the muscles after the turn. The tensed muscle is now able to impart speed to the clubhead, despite the short distance available. There is the obvious risk that, if the swing is too fast, you may be able to turn only the movement in your shoulders but not in your wrists. This results in your hands arriving over the ball before the clubhead reaches it, so that you top or slice. The remedy for this is increased flexibility in the back and shoulders, and increased strength in the muscles of the lower arms.

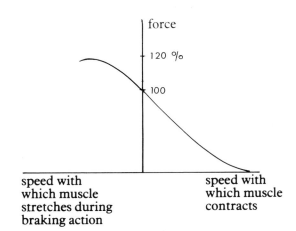

force

120 %

100

speed with which muscle stretches during braking action

speed with which muscle contracts

A muscle is at its strongest when it is stretched 20% more than its length at rest and then is forced to "put the brakes on" and change the movement to one that is going in the opposite direction (e.g. a backswing) to the desired one (downswing).

Warming up
Take any five of these exercises per warming-up session.

Jogging in the one position for 1 minute.

Jogging with knees as high as possible for 20 seconds.

"Draw" small circles in the air for 25 seconds. Then draw larger circles. Do this clockwise and anticlockwise.

Raise and lower your shoulders quickly for about 15 seconds.

Pass the driver, with your arms straight, forward and backward over your head for 20 seconds.

Pull your elbow down behind your head as shown for 15 seconds. Then change arms.

Stretch as far left as possible for 10 seconds. Then to the right.

"Swim" with the breast stroke or crawl for 30 seconds. Bend your knees.

With upper body bent forward, swing to the left for 20 seconds. Then to the right.

Swivel the upper body to the right for 30 seconds. Then to the left.

BIBLIOGRAPHY

Cochran, Alistair and Stobbs, John. *The Search for the Perfect Swing*. London, William Heinemann Ltd., 1968.

Getchell, Bud. *Being Fit—a personal guide*. New York, John Wiley & Sons Inc., 1982.

Jacobs, John. *Curing Faults for Weekend Golfers*. New York, Simon & Schuster, Inc., 1979.

Kostis, Peter. *The Inside Path to Better Golf*. New York, Simon & Schuster, Inc., 1982.

Maltby, Ralph. *Golf Club Design, Fitting, Alteration, and Repair*. Newark, Ohio, 1974.

Nicklaus, Jack. *Jack Nicklaus Playing Lessons*. London, Pan Books Ltd., 1981.

Railo, Willi. *Bäst när det gäller*. Stockholm, Svenska Idrottsförbund, 1983.

Rotella, Robert J. and Bunker, Linda K. *Mind Mastery for Winning Golf*. Englewood Cliffs, N.J., Prentice-Hall, Inc., 1981.

Toski, Bob and Flick, Jim. *How to Become a Complete Golfer*. New York, Simon & Schuster, Inc., 1978.

Wiren, Gary and Coop, Richard. *The New Golf Mind*. New York, Simon & Schuster, Inc., 1978.

Wirhed, Rolf. *Athletic Ability & the Anatomy of Motion*. London, Wolfe Medical, 1984.

INDEX

A

address 11 14 16 22 30 45
    56 102 103
    putting 69 – 71
angle of approach, clubhead
    36 39
Art of Golf, The 7
Augusta National golf
    course 115

B

backspin 46 52 53 81 84 85
    86 87 88 89 90 91 107
backswing 13 19 20 26 – 27
    32 96 100
ball carry 118
ball flight principles 35 – 64
ball roll 100 118

C

Carr, Joe 48
carry, length of 118
chipping 83 – 92 111 112
    club choice 83 84 85 86 87
      88 89 90 91 92
club 9 31
    blade 61
    length 31 32
    lie 67 104
    loft 31 101 102 103

clubface
    angle 42 43 48
    position 57
clubhead
    arc 33 36 38 39 55 105
    path *see* swing path
concentration 130 – 132
course management
    111 – 115
    knowing the course
    120 – 122

D

distance *see* **length of shot**
downswing 23 26 27 28 100
draw (hook) 51 112

E

elasticity, muscle 133
    152 – 153
exercises 136 – 151

F

fade (slice) 37 41 51 58 61
    104 111 112
fault analysis and correction
    55 – 60

fitness 133 148 – 149
flexibility 133 – 140
    test your 134 – 135
    exercises for 136 – 140

G

**Golf Society of Great
    Britain, The** 7 8 36 62
golf swing 7 – 8
    backswing 26 – 27 36 56 62
    building program 9 – 34
    downswing 23 26 – 28 36
      56 63
    full 25 – 30 32 33 34 36 48
    half backswing 21 – 24 34
      48
    power 62 – 63
    putting (pendulum) 9 – 15
    short swing 11 – 18
    wooden club 31 – 34
green, putting
    reading the 72 – 73
    types of 74
grip 58 60
    baseball 20 21
    "finger-over" 56
    Nicklaus 20 21
    putting 68 – 69
    "starter" 14 – 15
    Vardon 20 21

H

Hagen, Walter 131
half backswing 21 – 24
hook 37

I

impact angle 42 – 43
iron clubs
    clubhead arc 33 40
    length of shot 32
    loft 31

J

judging length 118 120

K

knowing the course
    120 – 122

L

length of shot 40 43 55 59
    117 118 125
lie of ball 80 – 81 82 84 85 86
    87 88 89 90 91 107 – 109
    downhill lies 106
    sidehill lies 103 – 105

    uneven lies 102 – 106
    uphill lies 105 – 106
lining up 44 – 45 59 60
loft 31 36 43 46 52 81 83
    sand club 94 – 95

M

Maltby, Ralph 95
mental game, your 115
    123 – 132
mental training sessions
    126 – 127
mis-hits 38 39 40 41 42 43 64
muscles, your golfing
    62 – 64 137 138 141
        152 – 153
    endurance training 141
        145
    flexibility 133 – 140
    speed training 141 145
    strength 141 – 145

N

nerves, golfing 129
Nicklaus, Jack 20 35 111

O

out of bounds 115

P

par 119
Pelz, Dave 74
physical fitness 133 – 155
pitching 87 88 89 90 91 106
    111 112
planning your round
    115 – 118
playing profile, defining
    your 112
positive thinking 124 – 127
practice 14 24 25 34 46 – 48
    52 76 – 77
    journal 47 48
problems and solutions
    55 – 60
progress chart 114
pull 51 64
pull-hook 51
pull-slice 51
push 51 54
push-slice 50 51
putting 9 – 15 65 – 76 79 – 80
    82
    address 68 – 71
    grip 68 – 70
    practice 76 – 77
    principles of 66 – 68
    reading the green 74 – 75
    routine 78

R

Rankin, Judy 60
reading the green *see* **putting**
**relaxation and problem
    solution** 126 – 127
rhythm 9 19 30
rough
    bad lies 109
    good lies 107
    half-good lies 107
    play from 107 – 110
round analysis 112 – 114
round planning 115 – 118
round summary 112 –113
running 147 – 148

S

sand, play from
    address positions 102 103
    choice of clubs 95 97 101
    long shots 100 – 102
    shot technique adjust-
        ments 102
    standard shots 96 – 97
    variations 98 – 99
    various lies 100 – 102
sand wedge 94 – 97
    selection table 95
    sole design 95 – 97
**Search for the Perfect
    Swing, The** 7 62 – 63
short game 79 – 92

ball-lie analysis and club
    choice 82 – 92
short swing 16 – 18
shot distance 19 32 43 61
sidespin 42 46 48 88
Simpson, Sir Walter 7 8
single-lever movement 18
    19 79 80 85 86 92
slice (fade) 37 41 51 104 111
    112
sole 94 95 104
    bounce 94 95
strength training 141 – 151
stress 129 – 130
stretching exercises 137
sweetspot 12 18 31 36 39 42
    66 – 67
swing centre point 20 39 40
    54 55 60 64 103 104
swing development *see* **golf
    swing**
swing path 36 38 39 40 41 48
    58

T

target line 40 41 42 44 45 49
    56 57 60
target-area analysis 81
thinned strike 38 39 52 64 92
    102 104
timing 27 61
topped shot 36 38 39 48

52 – 54 64 102 104
training *see* **practice**
trajectory 40 105 106 118
Trevino, Lee 115
two-lever movement 19 32
    79 88 90 93

V

Vardon, Harry 20

W

warming up 46 154 – 155
Watson, Tom 35
wood shots 30 – 34
wooden-club swing 31 – 34
    swing technique adjust-
        ments 31

*This book has been printed on 135 gsm matt-coated
paper by Grafedit Spa, Azzano S.P., Bergamo,
by arrangement with Graphicom, Vicenza, Italy.*